THE PATH OF
PRAYER

THE PATH OF
PRAYER

Samuel Chadwick

former principal,
Cliff College, Sheffield, England

CLC ❖ PUBLICATIONS
Fort Washington, Pennsylvania 19034

Published by CLC ❖ Publications

U.S.A.
P.O. Box 1449, Fort Washington, PA 19034

GREAT BRITAIN
51 The Dean, Alresford, Hants. SO24 9BJ

AUSTRALIA
P.O. Box 419M, Manunda, QLD 4879

NEW ZEALAND
10 MacArthur Street, Feilding

ISBN 0-87508-578-4

Contents

Chapter   Page

    About the Author 7

    Foreword 11

1. The Sign of Prayer 13

2. Learning to Pray 19

3. Praying in Secret 27

4. The Inner Room and the Closed Door 33

5. The Word of God and Prayer 39

6. Praying in the Name 51

7. Praying in the Spirit 57

8. Praying to God Our Father 63

9. The Importunity of Prayer 69

10. The Recompense of Prayer 77

11. The Power of Prayer 85

12. Praying and the Commonplace 95

13. The Prayer of Faith 103

14. Praying "One for Another" 109

15. Praying for Divine Healing 117

16. The Problem of Unanswered Prayer 125

About the Author

Preacher burns his sermons—
then catches fire himself!

SAMUEL CHADWICK was zealous for Jesus, but God had more in store for him: the power of the Holy Spirit's fire!

Samuel Chadwick was born in the industrial north of England in 1860. His father worked long hours in the cotton mill, and when he was only eight Samuel went to work there too, as a means of supporting the impoverished family.

Devout Methodists, they attended chapel three times on Sunday, and as a young boy Chadwick gave his heart to Christ. Listening to God's Word week by week, he often felt the inner call to serve Christ. It seemed impossible, as he was poor and uneducated; but in faith he made preparations. After a twelve-hour factory shift he would rush home for five hours of prayer and study.

At the age of 21 he was appointed lay pastor of a chapel at Stacksteads, Lancashire. It was no dream appointment; the congregation was self-satisfied. Yet Chadwick threw himself in with great optimism. He had been trained to prepare well-researched and interesting sermons as the sure way to bring in the crowds. He recalled later: "This led unconsciously to a false aim in my work. I lived and labored for my sermons, and was unfortunately more concerned about their excellence and reputation than the repentance of the people."

Soon, however, his sermons were exhausted and nothing had changed. Staring defeat in the face and sensing his lack of real power, he felt an intense hunger kindled within him for more of God. At this point he heard the testimony of someone who had been revitalized by an experience of the Holy Spirit, so with a few friends he covenanted to pray and search the Scriptures until God sent revival.

One evening as he was praying over his next sermon, a powerful sense of conviction settled on him. His pride, blindness and reliance on human methods paraded before his eyes as God humbled him to the dust. Well into the night he wrestled and repented, then he got out his pile of precious sermons and set fire to them! The result was immediate: the Holy Spirit fell upon him. In his own words: "I could not explain what had happened, but it was a bigger thing than I had ever known. There came into my soul a deep peace, a thrilling joy, and a new sense of power. My mind was quickened. I felt I had received a new faculty of understanding. Every power was vitalized. My body was quickened. There was a new sense of spring and vitality, a new power of endurance, and a strong man's exhilaration in big things."

The tide turned. At his next sermon seven souls were converted ("one for each of my barren years"), and he called the whole congregation to a week of prayer. The following weekend most of the church was baptized in the Holy Spirit and revival began to spread through the valleys. In the space of a few months hundreds were converted to Jesus, among them some of the most notorious sinners in the area.

The pattern was repeated over the next few years as Chadwick moved to various places. 1890 saw him in Leeds, where the power of God was so strongly upon him that the chapel was full half an hour before the service began, and police had to control the crowds. The river of God moved strongly, and Chadwick records: "We were always praying and fighting [the devil], singing and rejoicing, doing the impossible and planning still bigger things. The newspapers never left us alone, and people came from far and wide."

Opposition was swept away and within a few years the chapel had to be demolished and a substantial church built.

Always a man of the people, Chadwick would spend his Saturdays mixing with local workers. Once, when his wife was away, he teasingly invited anyone who was lonely to come for Saturday tea. He expected about a dozen. Six hundred turned up! Yet God had catered: one church member was a baker and had been awakened by the Lord with the order to bake for all he was worth!

The final phase of Chadwick's life was spent as Principal of Cliff College, a Methodist training school for preachers, and it was here that he wrote his famous book *The Way to Pentecost*, which was being printed when he died in 1932. In it we read: "I owe everything to the gift of Pentecost. For fifty days the facts of the gospel were complete, but no conversions were recorded. Pentecost registered three thousand souls. It is by fire that a holy passion is kindled in the soul, whereby we live the life of God. The soul's safety is in its heat. Truth without enthusiasm, morality without emotion, ritual without soul, make for a Church without power."

"Destitute of the Fire of God, nothing else counts;
possessing Fire, nothing else matters."

Foreword

IN SENDING forth this book on prayer a word of explanation is due. The chapters were written for *Joyful News*, and appeared as devotional meditations during Lent. That explains everything except why they are now published in book form, and that is because of the persistent urging by those to whom they were made a blessing. They were never intended for a book. They were written for the sole purpose of helping *Joyful News* readers in the life and ministry of prayer.

The Joyful News Mission was born of the prayers of Thomas and Mary Champness fifty years ago, as they prayed one morning between the hours of four and five. It has lived and worked by prayer ever since, and is itself a witness to the teaching of this book concerning the power of prayer. The relation of editor and readers has always been intensely personal and affectionately intimate. That explains the homely and practical intimacy of the articles. They were not written for critics nor for scholars, but for plain people who are deeply religious and sincerely simple in their trust. Hundreds of these readers wrote me grateful letters and begged that the articles should be put into a book. In the glow of their appreciation I promised that they would be, and then became shy of my promise. If they had been written for becoming a book the approach and treatment would have been different, but they might have lost the artlessness of a simple purpose. They are sent forth in the form in which it pleased God to bless them. No one can be more conscious of their limitations than I. Of one thing I am confident: I have written out of an honest heart that has sought above all things to be effectual in the communion and ministry of prayer, and to which there has come no greater joy than the fellowship of the inner sanctuary.

I have no knowledge of the sources to which I am indebted. I have nothing that I have not received, but I have kept no commonplace book, and have quoted sparingly. For more than fifty years I have read widely in the devotional literature of the mystics and the disciplines of religious orders; but I have written out of the experience of my own prayer life, in the hope that what has helped me may be helpful to others.

Samuel Chadwick
Cliff College, Calver,
Sheffield, England
August 21, 1931

1

The Sign of Prayer

ALL religions pray. God and prayer are inseparable. Belief in God and belief in prayer are elemental and intuitive. The ideas may be crude and cruel in primitive and pagan peoples, but they belong to the universal intuitions of the human race.

The teaching of the Old Testament is full of the subject of prayer. Everywhere there are commands and inducements to pray, and the great stories of deliverance and victory, experience and vision, are all examples of prevailing prayer.

In the Gospels, all the crises in the life of our Lord were linked with special seasons of prayer, and His teaching set forth wonderful assurances to those who pray. He laid down the laws of prayer, though He never sought to explain its mystery. Prayer was not a problem to Him. The two parables He spoke about prayer are not very acceptable, however, to those who pray. There is something alien to the spirit of prayer in likening God to a heartless judge (Luke 18:1–8) or a churlish friend (Luke 11:5–8). God is neither. The parables were not spoken as representative of God but to illustrate the reward of persistence.

The basis of prayer is sonship. Prayer is possible and reasonable because it is filial. It is natural for a child to ask something of its father, and it is reasonable for the father to listen to the request of his child. "If ye, then, being evil, know how to give good gifts unto your children, how much more shall your Father which is in heaven give good things to them that ask Him" (see Matt. 7:7–11). There are many problems about prayer, but they lie outside the fact and experience of prayer, and apart from praying there is no solution to them. Prayer is a fact of experience, and through all the ages the testimony of those who prayed has been that God hears and answers the prayer of His children.

What God Thinks About Prayer

The thoughts of God are not as man's thoughts, neither are His ways as man's ways. As the heavens are higher than the earth, so are God's ways higher than man's ways and His thoughts than man's thoughts (see Isa. 55:8–9). God has made known His thoughts and His ways in the revelation of His Word and in the Person of His Son. The medium of the revelation is experience, and the occasion is in the events of life in individuals and in history. God has never put His thoughts into a thesis of philosophy or metaphysics. He has interpreted them in life and set forth His ways in precepts, principles, and example.

There is one incident which most gloriously tells us what God thinks of prayer. Admittedly, God's mind concerning prayer is seen in every command to pray, in every law of prayer, in every promise concerning prayer, and in every example of answered prayer; every part is part of the whole. But every subject of Scripture has its final and complete expression, and in the conversion of Saul of Tarsus (Acts 9) there is a unique revelation of the mind of God concerning prayer. There are three persons in that incident of prayer. There is the man who prayed, the God who heard, and the man through whom the answer came. God, of course, is central. It is to Him prayer is made, through Him prayer is interpreted, and by Him prayer is answered.

God speaks of prayer in terms of wonder: "Behold, he prayeth" (v. 11). The language here is that of humanity, but it is the only speech man knows, and however inadequate it may be it stands for corresponding reality in God. Can God wonder? Can there be in Him elements of surprise and amazement? Can it be that there are things that to God are wonderful? That is how God speaks, and to Him there is nothing more gloriously wonderful than prayer. It would seem as if the biggest thing in God's universe is a man who prays. There is only one thing more amazing, and that is—that man, knowing this, should *not* pray. *Behold!* In that word there is wonder, rapture, exultation. In the estimate of God prayer is more wonderful than all the wonders of the heavens, more glorious than all the mysteries of the earth, more mighty than all the forces of creation.

God interprets prayer as a sign of all that happened to Saul of Tarsus on the Damascus road. The event is variously expressed. To the churches of Judea, it was a conversion that turned their arch-persecutor into a preacher. This is how Paul the apostle states it in writing to the Galatians: "Afterwards I came into the regions of Syria and Cilicia; and was unknown by face unto the churches of Judea which were in Christ: but they had heard only, He which persecuted us in times past now preacheth the faith which once he destroyed. And they glorified God in me" (Gal. 1:21–24). That is a conversion that was the result of an experience. What was the experience? Paul says that in the experience "it pleased God to reveal His Son in me" (v. 16). That is what the Damascus road experience meant to him. When God speaks of it He sums it all up in the words *"Behold, he prayeth."*

That is what it meant to God, and that is what it *always* means to Him. Prayer is the symbol and proof and gauge of grace. All that happens in the converting work of grace whereby we receive the adoption of sons is that, being sons, we begin to pray. Saul of Tarsus had been a praying man all his life, but it was not until then that he began to pray as *God* interprets prayer. The children's hymn is equally applicable to grown-up people:

> " I often say my prayers,
>   But do I ever pray?"

Prayer is the privilege of sons and the test of sonship. It would seem as if God divided all men into the simple classification of those who pray and those who do not. It is a very simple test, but it is decisive and divisive.

The Way God Answers Prayer

God answers joyously. There is a ring of exultation in the words He speaks to Ananias, like the joyous ring of our Lord's parables of the Lost Sheep, the Lost Coin, and the Lost Son. Rejoice with Me! "Behold, he prayeth!" There is joy in the heart of God the Father when His lost children begin to pray. He answers like the God He is. Ananias may parley with God, but God never parleys with man. The answering hand of God waits for the lifted hand of man, and the heart that answers always transcends the heart that cries.

The answer to Saul of Tarsus was twofold: God gave Saul a vision and sent a messenger—a vision and a man, each corresponding to the other. That is God's way: first an assurance and then the confirmation. That is the prayer of faith that never fails. God's servants are partners with Him in the ministry of prayer. That is the mystery of spiritual co-operation! The Lord goes before the man He sends. Saul was prepared and waiting for the man he had already seen in a vision of God! Ananias found Saul prepared and waiting.

God gave Ananias the sign of prayer as the proof of grace. It was His own sign, and it is the sign He still gives! Is there any proof that a man is a man of God like the fact that he is a man of prayer? Of Elijah it is said that he "prayed in his prayer" (James 5:17, A.V. margin). Of some men it is said that they live in an atmosphere of devotion; but it is one thing to live in an atmosphere of prayer and another to " pray in our praying." Finney went to a weekly prayer meeting where they prayed much and got no answers. Müller prayed and answers came, and that is why all men believed him to be a man of God. When I was a very small boy, not more than six or seven years of age, I was sent on an errand to the house of a neighbor named Davenport; it was about nine o'clock in the morning. I knocked, lifted the latch, and stepped inside. On the hearth, kneeling at a chair on which was an open Bible, was Mrs. Davenport, praying. She was unaware of my presence. I stood in silent awe for a moment, and then quietly stepped out and closed the door. It is more than sixty years since that morning, but from then till now I have known that Mrs. Davenport was a saint of God—because she prayed. It is God's infallible sign, and it is the only sign that even the world accepts as an infallible proof.

Prayer made all the difference to Saul of Tarsus, and it always makes all the difference. It brought a new assurance of God, a new confirmation of faith, a new fellowship of the people of God, a new experience of healing, a new vocation, a new inheritance, a new power. Prayer changes things. Prayer makes all things possible, for it links the praying soul to the omnipotence of God. Do we pray? Do we pray in our praying? Does God put His seal on our prayers?

Lord, teach us to pray!

> Prayer is the contrite sinner's voice
> Returning from his ways,
> While angels in their songs rejoice,
> And cry, Behold he prays.
>
> Prayer is the Christian's vital breath,
> The Christian's native air,
> His watchword at the gates of death,
> He enters heaven with prayer.

2

Learning to Pray

CAN PRAYER be learned? Is it not of the very soul of prayer that it shall be in the freedom of the Spirit? John the Baptist gave his disciples a form of prayer, and so the disciples of Jesus asked to be taught to pray (Luke 11:1). (There were not many things they asked Him to do for them, and when they did they were usually wrong.) Would He have given them a form of prayer if they had not asked Him? Why did they ask? Jesus' own praying awoke within them, it seems, a desire to be able to pray, and when they wanted to pray they found they did not know how. They obviously felt the need of some ordered form by which they could speak out of their heart to God. They quoted John for support.

There are still disciples who, in effect, quote John the Baptist to Jesus. Forms are easier than a creative spirit. Prayers counted on a rosary are easier than the prayers of a soul poured out in unrestrained speech to God. The Prayer Book helps the inarticulate to clearly express themselves. Such praying may be perfectly sincere, and the devout may find in provided prayers a real help to devotion, for it may be that such praying needs to be learned at the feet of instructors. Indeed, that *is* the kind of prayer that needs to be learned. The rosary prayers are simply recited; and morning and evening prayers in the Book of Common Prayer—though a non-Anglican might have difficulty finding his way—are uplifting and didactic. In fact, all praying begins with forms of prayer. There is hardly a soul who does not remember the simple, earnest prayers repeated at his mother's knee with reverent wonder and joy.

Personality in Prayer

It is not other people's prayers that make a man of prayer. All true prayer, the prayer that prevails, is personal, intimate, and original. Hannah protested that she had poured out her soul to God. That is prayer, and yet it is not the whole of prayer. Receptivity is as real a part of prayer as expression. Saul of Tarsus had been a praying man from his youth, but he never really prayed till he met the Risen Lord on the Damascus road. From the heavenward side the whole change that had been wrought was summed up in the words: "Behold, he prayeth."

The secret of Elijah's power in prayer was that he "prayed in his prayer." That is the translation given in the margin of the Authorized Version. He "prayed earnestly" is given in the text, and "fervently" in the Revised Version, with the note in the margin that says the Greek literally is "with prayer." He prayed with prayer; he prayed in his prayer. That is to say, he really prayed his prayers. He did not *say* prayers; he *prayed* in praying. His whole personality was in his supplication. He really wanted what he asked and fervently meant what he said. Can that kind of prayer be taught?

It is the prayer that prevails. Formal routine of temple service and the regular reading of words of secondhand inspiration and no understanding are neither acceptable to God nor profitable to man. They are vain repetitions. There is much praying that avails nothing, so far as we can judge. During the Baccarat Scandal, W. T. Stead computed the number and value of the prayers offered every day in the Anglican Church for the Prince of Wales, and the computation of value was not in proportion to their number. He was probably wrong, for prayer is not accounted in terms of arithmetic. The real problem is not there. Prayers are measured neither by time nor by number, but by intensity. There are prayers that are impassioned and there is no answer, and there are things for which we know we ought to pray in an agony of prayer and there is no power to pray. We do not know how to pray.

Prayer Learned by Praying

There is no way to learn to pray but by praying. No reasoned philosophy of prayer ever taught a soul to pray. The subject is beset with problems, but there are no problems of prayer to the man who prays! They are all met in the fact of answered prayer and the joy of fellowship with God. We know not what we should pray for as we ought, and if prayer waits for understanding it will never begin. We live by faith. We walk by faith. Edison wrote in 1921: "We don't know the millionth part of one percent about anything. We don't know what water is. We don't know what light is. We don't know what gravitation is. We don't know what enables us to keep on our feet when we stand up. We don't know what electricity is. We don't know what heat is. We don't know anything about magnetism. We have a lot of hypotheses about these things, but that is all. But we do not let our ignorance about all these things deprive us of their use." We discover by using. We learn by practice. Though a man should have all knowledge about prayer, and though he understand all mysteries about prayer, unless he prays he will never learn to pray.

There have been souls that were mighty in prayer, and they *learned* to pray. There was a period in their lives when they were as others in the matter of prayer, but they became mighty with God and prevailed. In every instance there was a crisis of grace, but it was in the discipline of grace that they discovered the secret of power. They were known as men of God because they were men of prayer. Some of them were re-named, like Jacob and Simon and Saul. They were called "Praying John," "Praying Mary," "Praying Bramwell," and "Praying Hyde." Our Methodist Fathers were mighty in prayer. They saved England by prayer. They shook the gates of hell by prayer. They opened the windows of heaven by prayer. How did they learn to pray? They learned to pray by being much in prayer. They did not talk about prayer; they prayed. They did not argue about prayer; they prayed.

Trained in Prayer

Prayer touches infinite extremes. It is so simple that a little child can pray, and it is so profound that none but a child-heart can pray. Montgomery's hymn has immortalized its profound simplicity:

> Prayer is the soul's sincere desire,
>   Uttered or unexpressed,
> The motion of a hidden fire
>   That trembles in the breast.
>
> · · · · · ·
>
> Prayer is the simplest form of speech
>   That infant lips can try;
> Prayer the sublimest strains that reach
>   The Majesty on High.

That is gloriously true. A cry brings God. A cry is mightier than the polished phrase. The Pharisee prayed within himself. His prayers revolved on ruts of vanity in his own mind and heart. The publican cried and was heard. It is not of emergency exits of the soul that we are thinking but the sustained habit and experience of the man of prayer. Such prayer comes by training, and there is no discipline so exacting. Coleridge says of such praying that it is the very highest energy of which the human heart is capable, and it calls for the total concentration of all the faculties. The great mass of worldly men and learned men he pronounced incapable of prayer. To pray as God would have us pray is the greatest achievement of earth.

Such a life of prayer costs. It takes time. Hurried prayers and muttered litanies can never produce souls mighty in prayer. Learners give hours regularly every day that they may become proficient in art and mechanism. Our Lord rose before daybreak that He might pray, and not infrequently He spent all night in prayer. All praying saints have spent hours every day in prayer. One is afraid to quote examples. In these days there is no time to pray; but without time, and a lot of it, we shall never learn to pray. It ought to be possible to give God one hour out of twenty-four all to Himself. Anyway, let us make a start in the discipline of training in prayer by setting apart a fixed time every day for the exercise of prayer. We must seriously set our hearts to learn how to pray. "Believe me, to pray with all your heart and strength, with the reason and the will, to believe vividly that God will listen to your voice through Christ, and verily do the thing He pleaseth thereupon—this is the last, the greatest achievement of the Christian's warfare upon earth."

Teach us to pray, O Lord, we beseech Thee.

> The praying Spirit breathe,
>   The watching power impart,
> From all entanglements beneath,
>   Call off my anxious heart.
>
> My feeble mind sustain,
>   By worldly thoughts oppressed,
> Appear, and bid me turn again
>   To my eternal rest.

When you feel the strain of discipline remember these words:

> . . . Thou art oft most present, Lord,
>   In weak, distracted prayer;
> A sinner out of heart with self,
>   Most often finds Thee there.

For prayer that humbles sets the soul
   From all delusions free,
And teaches it how utterly
   Dear Lord, it hangs on Thee.

3

Praying in Secret

LEARNING to pray is no light undertaking. If prayer is the greatest achievement on earth, we may be sure it will call for a discipline that corresponds to its power. The school of prayer has its conditions and demands. It is a forbidden place to all but those of set purpose and resolute heart. Strong men often break down under the strain of study. Concentration here is a heavier task than handling a hammer or guiding a plow. The discipline curbs freedom, and drills the mind to attention. Understanding is more taxing than doing, and meditation is a severer tax than service.

The reason so many people do not pray is because of its cost. The cost is not so much in the sweat of agonizing supplication as in the daily fidelity to the life of prayer. It is the acid test of devotion. Nothing in the life of faith is so difficult to maintain. There are those who resent the association of discipline and intensity with prayer. They do not pray like that, and certainly they would not like their children to entreat and plead for anything they wanted with "strong crying and tears." This aversion to tears is quite understandable—but then no one suspects them of praying like that, and the analogy of their children may not be the whole truth. Nothing can be farther from the truth than a false analogy. The school of prayer is for those who really want to learn to pray.

The Secret Place

Those who come to learn are disciples. They put themselves under the yoke of Him from whom they seek to learn, and the first condition of learning is a teachable spirit. Our Lord has the authority to teach, and He Himself is Example as well as Instructor. There is no appeal beyond Him. Having besought Him to teach us how to pray, we surrender mind and heart to His teaching and yield all to the discipline of loyal and believing obedience.

What does our Lord teach us as to prayer?

One of the first things He commands is that there shall be a *place* of prayer. It is quite true that the whole earth is the Lord's, and that there is no place where prayer may not be heard. God wills that men should pray everywhere. Wherever we may be, He is nigh at hand and not afar off, and wherever there is a praying heart, the soul finds the sanctuary of God. No one would suggest that Jesus did not appreciate the sacredness of all the earth—which He said was the footstool of God—but it was His habit to withdraw into a solitary place to pray. He needed the fenced spaces of silence. To His disciples He said:

"And when ye pray, ye shall not be as the hypocrites: for they love to stand and pray in the synagogues and in the corners of the streets, that they may be seen of men. Verily I say unto you, They have received their reward. But thou, when thou prayest, enter into thine inner chamber, and having shut thy door, pray to thy Father which is in secret, and thy Father which seeth in secret shall recompense thee" (Matt. 6:5–6).

Why does He insist upon this inner chamber and the closed door? The first reason is that the first quality God requires in prayer is reality. Hypocrites never pray in secret. Prayers that are a pretense require an audience. They are intended to be heard of men, and they have their reward in skill of phrasing, a show of earnestness, and a reputation for piety. These things do not count with God. They cannot live in His presence. Prayer is between the soul and God alone.

The Silent Spaces of the Soul

The soul needs its silent spaces. It is in them we learn to pray. There, alone, shut in with God, our Lord bids us pray to our Father who is in the secret place and who sees in secret. There is no test like solitude. Fear takes possession of most minds in the stillness of the solitary place. The heart shrinks from being alone with God who sees in secret! Who shall abide in His presence? Who can dwell with God who is shadowless light? Hearts must be pure and hands clean that dare shut the door and be alone with God. It would revolutionize the lives of most men if they were shut in with God in some secret place for half an hour a day.

For such praying all the faculties of the soul need to be awake and alert. When our Lord took Peter and James and John with Him to the secret place of prayer, they were heavy with sleep. It was the same on the Mount of Glory and in the Garden of Agony, and it was not until they were fully awake that they saw the glory or realized the anguish. There are some silent places of rare wisdom where men may not talk but they find it possible to sleep. Daydreaming is not meditation, and drowsy repose is not praying. The secret place of prayer calls for every faculty of mind and heart.

> " Bless the Lord, O my soul;
>   And all that is within me
>   Bless His Holy Name."

As for praise, so for prayer the whole being is called. There is a vital difference between private and corporate prayer. Each kind of prayer brings blessing after its kind, but there is a difference. Corporate prayer is less exacting. There is a sense of fellowship that gives courage and inspires expression. Guided prayer is companionable, but it has a tendency to do its thinking by proxy. In private prayer the soul stands naked and alone in the presence of God. Thought is personal, prayer is original, motive is challenged. Corporate prayer gives a spirit of fellowship; private prayer disciplines personality. Who can measure the influence of an hour a day spent alone with God?

The Hill of the Lord

The way into the Holy Presence is not a

thoroughfare. The inner chamber into which a man goes is his own, but it is the Presence of God that makes it a holy place. To a secular mind there would be no Presence. It is the seeking soul that finds. There are some people to whom no audience is given. There are souls that cannot pray. James says of some men that they need not think they can receive anything of the Lord. Even before Christ taught men to pray, the Psalmist declared, "If I regard iniquity in my heart, the Lord will not hear" (Ps. 66:18). The Judgment Seat of God is in the inner chamber; but the Throne of Grace is there also, or none would ever dare to enter in. Forgotten sins start into life, and hidden things stand naked and open before Him with whom we have to do. All who would enter the Holy Presence and live must have a sincere desire for God and a conscience set on dwelling in the light.

Our Lord laid emphasis upon the forgiving spirit. The one thing above all others that bolts and bars the way into the "presence chamber" of prayer is unwillingness to forgive from the heart. No gift can be accepted by God until reconciliation has been made. "If therefore thou art offering thy gift at the altar, and there rememberest that thy brother hath aught against thee, leave there thy gift before the altar, and go thy way; first be reconciled to thy brother, and then come and offer thy gift" (Matt 5:23–24).

Again, when Jesus stated the law of faith in relation to prayer, He said: "Therefore I say unto you, All things whatsoever ye pray and ask for, believe that ye have received them, and ye shall have them. And whensoever ye stand praying, forgive, if ye have aught against any one; that your Father also which is in heaven may forgive you your trespasses. But if ye do not forgive, neither will your Father which is in heaven forgive your trespasses" (Mark 11:24–26).

Why did He lay such emphasis upon forgiveness? Was it not for the same reason that the Law and the Prophets placed the emphasis upon righteousness? All who would come to the Holy One must be holy, and whoever will come to the God of Mercy must be merciful. The petitioner for grace must believe in grace.

"Thine Inner Chamber"

Let no soul be discouraged from making a beginning. Schools are graded to the capacity of the learners. The great souls who became mighty in prayer and rejoiced to spend three and four hours a day alone with God were once beginners. They went from strength to strength. For our comfort let us remember that it is into our own inner chamber we enter, and the God who is there is our Father. Many years ago a sweet little girl stole into my bedroom in the house where I was staying. She prattled blithely over all the wonder of her child world, but when I asked if her father was up, she looked radiantly and reverently into my eyes and said, "Oh, my daddy always talks with God in the drawing room before breakfast."

Happy father! Happy child! Happy God!

4

The Inner Room and the Closed Door

"**B**UT thou, when thou prayest, enter into thine inner chamber, and having shut thy door, pray to thy Father which is in secret, and thy Father which seeth in secret shall recompense thee" (Matt. 6:6).

There are two difficulties awaiting us at the threshold of this command. One is that many have no inner chamber. There is no place in their lives for privacy. They have no room that is not shared, and if they could find room they have no leisure. The closed door may neither shut out nor shut in. The radio has made us familiar with the fact that neither bolted doors nor shuttered windows can secure privacy. Thought is more subtle than sound, and Satan is more cunning than the radio engineer. The saints who have been practiced in private prayer bear witness of the adversaries that keep watch at the door of the soul's inner chamber.

Where Shall We Find the Secret Place?

My aim is not to instruct but to suggest. Manuals
of devotion have usually been to me depressing rather
than helpful. They are either too mechanical or too
exacting. They discourage rather than inspire. I want
to write quite frankly, and in the first person. All my
life I have wanted to learn to pray. In my zeal I have
experimented and explored in likely and unlikely ways
and schools of prayer, and without pose or pride I want
in meekness and humility to tell you what I have
learned. I speak for myself. I judge no man's method,
criticize no man's counsel, challenge no man's experience. I speak with utmost simplicity, and you must
judge what I say.

Let us begin with the difficulty of privacy. There
are tens of thousands of Christ's disciples who have
no room to which they can retire for private prayer.
They live with other people, sleep with other people,
work with other people. They cannot escape from
people. Is not this a reason why the door of the house
of God should never be closed? One Monday morning
a penitent sinner stopped me in the main street of the
town where I had preached on the Sunday. There were
three nonconformist churches near at hand, but they
were locked and bolted, back and front, and we had
to go to the parish church to find a place where there
was privacy for prayer. The door of the church should
always be open. Even that does not meet the need of
the soul. The secret place of prayer should be part of
the daily life, a part of the daily dwelling place.

Some place must be found that shall be a trysting

place with God. A hungry heart will find a way. In the open air or in some secluded corner, some inner sanctuary will be found. If this advantage is impossible, the soul must make an open space into which it can withdraw, even in the presence of others, and be alone with God; but the "inner chamber" is an unspeakable boon. Happily, God wills that men should pray everywhere, but the place of His glory is in the solitudes, where He hides us in the cleft of the rock, and talks with man face to face as a man talks with his friend.

How Can We Secure the Closed Door?

How is it possible to keep the world from coming in and the mind from straying out? Concentration on any subject is a severe strain upon the mind, and nowhere is it so difficult as in the place and practice of private prayer. An enemy is there to raise bogies, excite conscience, jog memory, and direct invaders of the sacred hour. Some simple device will usually secure the secret place from intrusion. General Gordon pinned a white handkerchief at the opening of his tent. I hang a card outside the door when I wish to be alone. That is simple enough, but though it may keep people out it is useless against the distractions of the mind, and a body may just as well be roaming at large as be shut in with a wandering mind. How can the door be so shut as to keep out the things that divert and distract?

Attention is an act of the will. Concentration is sustained attention upon a specific object. The will can be disciplined and the power of concentration developed. An educated mind is trained to attention, discrimination, and concentration. By patience the soul is won, and by discipline the mind is trained. God is in secret. Let the first act be to affirm the fact of the Holy Presence. Call every faculty of mind and body to remembrance, recognition, and realization of the God who is in secret and sees in secret. Hold the mind to this fact. Tolerate no distraction, allow no diversion, indulge no dissipation. Every faculty must be alert. Of the apostles on the Holy Mount it is said they were heavy with sleep, but when they were fully awake they saw His glory. Dreaming is not meditation. Dozing is not thinking. Moping is not praying. Prayer in the secret place demands every faculty at its best.

Our Lord gave His disciples a form and order of prayer, and it does not begin with either song or supplication, but with the contemplation of God:

> Our Father,
> Which art in heaven,
> Hallowed be Thy name.

It is in this way all the great prayers of the Bible begin. That is how I find it helpful to begin. I think in adoring love and wonder of His character and attributes, of His majesty and might, of His grace and glory. Musing kindles the fire, and the flame becomes "a wall of fire round about" which keeps beasts and intruders at a safe distance. That is why I so often find that prayer in the secret place begins with the Doxology, and abounds in glory and thanksgiving. It is there the transfigured Lord is seen.

The Word of God in the Holy Presence

I never take any book but the Bible into the secret place. It is my prayer book. I seek no external aids to devotion, such as the Cross or Crucifix. I have no altar but the one within the veil. Other minds have other ways. Most people have some devotional classic, but I do not take even my hymn book. I will write more fully on the devotional use of the Bible, and at present I will content myself with saying that I feed upon it by searching its truth, appropriating its affirmations, and turning its psalms and prayers into personal thanksgiving and supplication. Questions of criticism, textual or otherwise, do not enter into my mind in the secret place, any more than questions of chemical analysis trouble me when I eat my dinner. The Word is more to me than my necessary food. It thrills and moves me with tremendous power.

The Word of God instructs us how to pray. The posture of the body must be determined by conditions of health and comfort. Normally, to kneel is reverent and helpful. One of my friends tells me that he sits, and close by him he places a vacant chair. The habit should be to kneel, but conditions of health and soul will dictate their own posture. It is fitting that we should "kneel before the Lord our Maker." Prayer is more than asking, but even our asking should be instructed under the direction of the Holy Spirit. I find it good to rehearse and review my daily life in the Holy Presence. It is there I make my plans. God keeps the pattern of earthly things in the Holy Mount. Thomas Champness talked with God about his work and his evangelists every morning from five to six. God guides with His eye, and eyes speak best in the place of secret communion. It is there we are assured of His will and are made to understand His way.

It is the place of Intercession. That is the place where we can talk freely with God about other people. The family, the church, the business, the friendships, the nation, the world, are all subjects of earnest and believing private prayer. Class leaders should go over the classbook name by name; the Sunday School superintendent over the teachers' roll, and the teacher over the class register in the same way, name by name. Keep a prayer list of subjects for intercession, and always have a list of people for whom you pray. It is not necessary to tell anyone else the things you tell to God. The Father is in secret, He sees in secret. He hears in secret; leave it to Him to make it known.

The God in secret is our Father. Prayer is filial; we pray as sons and daughters in the Father's house. He knows our need better than we can tell Him, and He is able to do exceeding abundantly above all we can ask or think; therefore ask in confidence, nothing doubting. It is in the secret place we learn that silence is the best speech and listening is the best part of praying. Those who speak are heard, and those who listen hear. Of Jesus it is said: "And in the morning, a great while before day, He rose up and went out, and departed into a desert place, and there prayed."

5

The Word of God
and Prayer

THE WORD of God quickens the soul and instructs it in prayer. The Psalmist speaks for all who pray when he confesses to seasons when the soul could not find its wings: "My soul cleaveth unto the dust; quicken Thou me according to Thy Word." It is always to the Word of God he turns for reviving and instruction. St. Paul links together the Word of God and prayer. "And take . . . the sword of the Spirit which is the Word of God; praying always with all prayer and supplication, and watching thereunto with all perseverance and supplication for all saints; and for me." Watching where and whereunto? Watching with all perseverance! That is surely with diligence and patience, alertness and reverence. We must search the Word, that we may know how to pray. "God is Spirit; and they that worship Him must worship Him in spirit and in truth."

Aids to Devotion

It must be remembered that I do not judge any man in the method of devotion. I speak only for myself. The practice of private prayer is so difficult to maintain that I grudge no help to those who find aids in things that to me would be a hindrance. Some find help in symbols and pictures, and most of those who seek to cultivate the prayer life of the soul keep some book of devotion at hand. Thomas à Kempis, Lancelot Andrewes, William Law, Andrew Murray, and the hymnology of all the churches have been blessed to tens of thousands who have sought to know how to pray. It may be a confession of shame, but I do not want any of them in the "inner chamber." I can appreciate them, more or less, elsewhere, but not here.

There are two perils to be avoided: one is emotional unreality; and the other is intellectual preoccupation. An earnest believer whose religious enthusiasm found expression in service for the Church and humanity was convicted of prayerlessness. He earnestly resolved to spend half an hour every day in private prayer. At the end of a month he gave it up because he could not endure the sense of unreality. He could not talk or meditate half an hour every day when there was no one there! There was not only no sense of a Presence, but there was a very real consciousness of an absence. There can be no experience of heart speech and soul fellowship without a consciousness of a Presence. The soul cannot keep up an emotional make-believe day after day. The mind cannot live in a vacuum. The Father is in secret, but it is the glory of His Presence that makes the sanctuary. There must be truth as well as spirit in all worship, and nowhere is the combination more necessary than in the secret place of prayer.

Altar fires are kindled and quickened by truth, but the truth must get to the altar. Devotional studies do not necessarily lead to devotion. There may be a preoccupation with truth that becomes an obsession. The study of experiential truth may never become experience, and the experience of others become a snare. Even the Bible may become a hindrance. Light can blind. Our Lord reproached the religious teachers of His day because their misuse of the Scriptures blinded their minds. Stepping-stones may become slipping-stones, and even a cornerstone may be a stumbling-block. In all questions of the soul each must find help where he can.

The Devotional Use of the Bible

Have we still got a Bible we can take into the Holy Place? The most disastrous result of paganizing the Bible is that it has so largely fallen into disuse as a book of devotion. An honest man cannot pray through a discredited book. Truth is as essential to man as to God. If he is to worship, he must worship in spirit and in truth. Some modernist teachers and preachers have what the learned call a "complex." The unlearned call it a "bee in the bonnet." They never miss a chance to drag in a jibe at what they call the traditional view of the Bible, and yet they insist that nothing has been lost in the change. The Scriptures are still "the living and sovereign Word of God." Even modernists admit that "Jesus took the Bible at its face value," and that in it He found His gospel, on it He fed His soul, and in all the great crises of His life relied upon its truth. The disciple may be content to be as his Lord.

There are methods of Bible study that do not belong to the inner sanctuary of prayer. Historical sources, literary criticism, higher criticism, and lower criticism belong to the forum and the study. They are concerned with the external conditions and progressive development of revealed truth. In the Holy Place the Scriptures are received as "the living, sovereign Word of God." How many so ever may be the inspired writers, there is but one Author. "Holy men of God spake as they were moved by the Holy Ghost." Questions of date, authorship, and the like are left outside, not because ignorance is more helpful to prayer than intelligence, but because they are irrelevant. In all Scripture there is a local and immediate message of truth, but there is also a revelation that is timeless and universal. Local knowledge is essential to complete understanding, but the soul in prayer comes to the Word that it may find God, and to the soul at prayer it is the infallible, sovereign, saving Word of God. Therefore we may still take the Scriptures into the inner chamber. Even the critics are anxious to assure us that the things for which they contend are not among the things that really matter, and, after all, their "assured results" are nothing more than "agreed hypotheses."

I do not want to harp unduly on the subject of Biblical criticism, but I think it may help you if I tell you how I regard the Scriptures. It always seems to me that there is a very real analogy between the Word of the Lord and the law of the land. The judge and jury accept the law, and it is their business not to criticize or amend but to interpret and administer. They have no concern with the politics and politicians by whom the law came. It is very interesting to study the historical situation it was intended to meet, to trace the agitation of the reformers, to know who framed the bill, and who was responsible for amending clauses, but that is the business of historians, experts, and antiquarians. Even a lawyer may be ignorant of them. His business is to *know* the law. The business of a judge is to *interpret* the law. The business of the jury is to submit their verdict to the *authority* of the law. So it is with the Word of God. There may be two Isaiahs or twenty, two contributors to the Pentateuch or two hundred, Mark's Gospel may have begun with "Q" or any other letter of the alphabet. The Word has passed beyond personal and historical limitations, and because of the Inspiration that gave them, the Scriptures are the Word of the Lord that abideth for ever. We take the Bible into the inner sanctuary, not that we may know what is its literary history, but that we may hear what the Lord our God will say unto us.

The Praying Method in the World

Paul said, "I will pray with the understanding also." The Word of God gives understanding to prayer. The Bible is not an easy book to the uninitiated, and that is why so many fall back upon ordered and simple

books of devotion, but *it* is the book of common prayer
to be understood by the common people. I think I can
help you best by telling you of my own method.

The first question is where to begin. Each will find
his own starting point. I begin with the Psalms. The
next thing to decide is the most suitable time of the
day. When I began I was called at five o'clock in the
morning, and had to be at work at six, so I read my
morning portion the night before. I read through the
appointed portion in a prayer spirit again and again,
then went over it clause by clause on my knees, turning
its statements into prayer and thanksgiving. Then I
wrote out the verse or phrase that spoke to me, read it
over next morning as I dressed, committed the day
briefly to God, and put the text in my waistcoat pocket.
Before I found this method I used to try to work myself
into a praying mood, but I lacked resourcefulness, and
praying became "prayers" again, and listening a void.
Prayer has been an experience of thrilling wonder,
creative meditation, and real fellowship since it has
been instructed, quickened, and inspired by the Word
of God.

In addition to this simple method, I find great help
in the use of the marginal references, especially those
of the Revised Version. The method taught by the
Holy Spirit is to compare scripture with scripture, and
spiritual things with spiritual. The Spirit who inspired
the Scriptures is given to us for interpretation. The
Holy Spirit and the Holy Word are never at variance.
Revelation is progressive, and every part has its relative
truth. To watch the unfolding of the Word deeply stirs
my soul. New discoveries excite the mind and kindle

the fires of worship and praise. Is this prayer? It assuredly is, so long as it is kept to its devotional purpose, and not followed with any other object. I once tried taking Scripture passages set for examination as my devotional portion, but it left the hour barren and unprofitable. God wants the whole presence of the spirit, as surely as man wants the sense of the real presence of God. The soul is never less alone than when it is alone with God.

How to Use the Word in Prayer

It is best to have no book but the Bible, that scripture may be interpreted by scripture. I find it well to take the sayings of Psalmist and prophet and turn them into prayers. Avoid the lure of sidetracks. I have been interested to find that men known far and wide for their Biblical scholarship always use the Authorized Version in their devotions. I commend their example. Search the Scriptures. The heart is soon aglow when the Word is alight.

The Word of God is like God's world: it is all interesting and all wonderful, but there are places to which we go often in thought and affection if not in actual visits: beauty spots of which we never tire, and sacred places of hallowed association. So there are pages of the Bible that wear thin with use, and some that are stained with tears. There is no Psalter like the Book of Psalms. There are favorite psalms that register the pilgrimage of the soul. I love the thirty-seventh, the forty-sixth, the eightieth, and the one hundred and sixteenth, and many more besides. Usually I read through the psalm, and then return for meditation to a few verses that have appealed to me. How often I have countered "fret" with "trust" in Psalm 37, committed my way unto the Lord, and hummed and prayed through the matchless words, "O rest in the Lord, and wait patiently for Him"; and my soul rejoices in the assurance that if I delight myself in the Lord, He will give me the desires of my heart. It is great to take the Lord's own words and speak them in praise and plead them in prayer.

The forty-sixth psalm is just as wonderful, with its three-fold division of catastrophe, hostility, and testimony. Then I go back to the first verse, with its description of God as Refuge, Strength, and Help. The Refuge is for sanctuary in perils in which man is utterly helpless. What can he do against a changing earth, hurtling mountains, and ranging storm? When sudden calamity comes and the foundations slip from under our feet, God is our Refuge. Other passages come to mind. "The eternal God is thy refuge, and underneath are the everlasting arms" (Deut. 33:27). Always underneath! Always lower than our deepest depths! God is also our Strength. There are demands for which we have no might and enemies against whom we have not strength. "He gives power to the faint, and to them that have no might He increaseth strength" (Isa. 40:29). Immediately the mind is among the heroes of God, and faith rejoices in the assurance of strength that shall be as the day. God is a Help. There are experiences in which we are incomplete. A Helper is near, companionable, encouraging, inspiring, achieving. Could assurance be more complete? No wonder the heart nestles near to God and whispers, "I will trust, and not be afraid."

> The Lord of Hosts is with *me*;
> And the God of Jacob is *my* refuge.

I wonder how often I have prayed through Psalm 116. It was one of God's earliest gifts to me. There is no need to change the pronoun, for there is a personal pronoun in every verse. I love the alternating surge of a sorrow escaped and the triumphant note of thanksgiving, and I linger long over the vows of the redeemed soul. He had been down into the depths. Every kind of trouble seemed to come at once, and greatest of all was his loss of faith in God and man. Deliverance came when he prayed. Praise followed prayer, and praise became a sacrifice of thanksgiving.

> "Return unto thy rest, O my soul;
> For the Lord hath dealt bountifully with thee.
> For Thou has delivered my soul from death,
> Mine eyes from tears,
> And my feet from falling.
> I will walk before the Lord
> In the land of the living."

There are scriptures that I read at stated seasons! One of my earliest attempts at real Bible study was to try to write out in order the doings and sayings of our Lord in the week of His Passion, and I go over those passages always in the Sacred Week! There are similar passages for Advent and other festivals of the Christian year! The first thing I do with a new Bible is to mark the passages in St. John in which our Lord makes His promise of the Paraclete, and those I read always between Easter and Pentecost, and then I find my inner chamber becomes my Lord's Upper Room.

There are three scriptures that I have read on fixed days of the week for more than forty years. Every Sunday morning I read the fifth chapter of Revelation, and every Sunday night the seventh chapter from verse 9. Why do I do this? Sunday is the great day of my week. I may preach on other days, but there is only one day in seven that is specially the Lord's Day. It is a day devoted to worship and the ministry of the Word. To me is given the responsibility of intercessor and prophet, teacher and evangelist. I have to represent Christ, preach Christ, plead for Christ. For all this I need the vision of Christ, and nowhere do I find the vision as He is there revealed in the midst of the Throne, in the midst of the redeemed, in the midst of the angels, and in the midst of creation. I can face the day when I have beheld His glory and said Amen, Hallelujah! in His presence. At night I come back to the vision of His ultimate triumph and commit the day unto Him and rest my heart within the veil.

On Monday morning I invariably read Isaiah 41. from verse 8. Monday morning is a difficult time for the prophet-evangelist. Sunday looks somber on Monday. A "blue Monday" is the devil's chance, so I resolved at the beginning of my ministry that if I had to have a blue Monday I would have it in the middle of the week, and God gave me this scripture as a protection against the "blues." Perhaps you would like to know how He did it. It was in my first month out of college. I was in my own room on a Monday morning, wrapped in a robe, for I had a cold and the room was cold. It rained pitilessly all the morning. Just before noon a cab stopped at the door, and H. S. B. Yates, the minister of Leith, was announced. We had only met twice. When I asked how he was, he answered, "I am a worm and no man." He had the blue Monday so badly that he had taken a cab and come to see me for a change. His church had been crowded the night before for the first time, and Satan taunted and tormented him into sheer terror. I listened with amused amazement. I am not made that way. He asked me what I did when I felt myself a creeping, crawling, contemptible worm? I had just read the forty-first of Isaiah, and I said, "Here is the very chapter for you. It is God's promise to a worm." We read it. We prayed through it, and he went away greatly comforted. Since then I have read it every Monday morning, and have found it a rare defense against depression, with the result that Monday has been one of my busiest and happiest days.

I go also through other portions of the Bible as I have gone through these passages of Scripture.

These are intimate words, but at any rate you do not wonder that to me the Word of the Lord is precious. All the time I have tried to keep in mind the overworked and toil-driven who have little or no space for an inner sanctuary. That is why I urge the Bible as the only necessary book for the devotional hour. For the same reason I advise that it be studied in short portions, lest prayer become secondary in the place consecrated to prayer.

6

Praying in the Name

THE MOST incredible things are promised to prayer. The Old Testament abounds in promises and examples. Deliverance and help, guidance and grace were assured to those who called upon God and committed their way unto Him. Nothing was too hard for the Lord, and nothing was impossible to those who prayed. Some of the passages are overwhelming in their challenge to prayer. Here is one: "Thus saith the Lord, the Holy One of Israel, and his Maker: Ask Me of the things that are to come; concerning My sons, and concerning the work of My hands, command ye Me" (Isa. 45:11). Prayer passes from entreaty to command.

There is no limit to the possibility of prayer, and the Old Testament confirms and attests the promises by examples and demonstrations of its power. Our Lord speaks with the same illimitable speech. His word is, "Ask, and it shall be given you; seek, and ye shall find; knock, and it shall be opened unto you: for every one that asketh receiveth; and he that seeketh findeth; and to him that knocketh it shall be opened" (Matt. 7:7–8). He gave prayer a new basis, a new confidence, and a new range. For He gave as its reason the fact that God is our heavenly Father. Prayer is a child's petition. "If ye, then, being evil, know how to give good gifts unto your children, how much more shall your Father which is in heaven give good things to them that ask Him" (Matt. 7:11). There is one saying of Jesus that is even more startling than that of Isaiah. "Therefore," says He, " I say unto you, What things soever ye desire, when ye pray, believe that ye receive them, and ye shall have them" (Mark 11:24).

"Whatsoever Ye Shall Ask in My Name"

The promise to prayer reaches its climax in the Upper Room on that memorable night of revelation and tragedy. He declared Himself to be the basis of prayer. They were to pray in a new way. They were to pray in His name, and they would be heard for His sake. As there are seven words on the Cross, so there are seven words concerning prayer in the fellowship of the Upper Room. They gather up and complete the whole revelation of the Scriptures, and enlarge and certify the promises of God. It would seem to be sacrilege not to quote them in full, for no other words can compare with them.

"And whatsoever ye shall ask in My name, that will I do, that the Father may be glorified in the Son. If ye shall ask anything in My name, I will do it" (John 14:13–14).

"If ye abide in Me, and My words abide in you, ye shall ask what ye will, and it shall be done unto you" (John 15:7).

"Ye did not choose Me, but I chose you, and appointed you, that ye should go and bear fruit, and that your fruit should abide: that whatsoever ye shall ask of the Father in My name, He may give it you" (John 15:16).

"And ye therefore now have sorrow: but I will see you again, and your heart shall rejoice, and your joy no one taketh away from you. And in that day ye shall ask Me no question [marg. R.V.]. Verily, verily, I say unto you, If ye shall ask anything of the Father, He will give it you in My name. Hitherto have ye asked nothing in My name: ask, and ye shall receive, that your joy may be full. . . . In that day ye shall ask in My name" (John 16:22–26).

What extraordinary promises these are that are pledged to prayer in the name of our Lord and Saviour Jesus Christ. They abound in universal and un-conditional terms. All things, whatsoever ye ask! Prayer reaches its highest level when offered in the name which is above every name, for it lifts the petitioner into unity and identity with our Mediator Himself.

"In the Name of Our Lord Jesus Christ"

Our Lord never explained what was meant by praying in His name. The meaning was plain enough to every Israelite. God had revealed Himself through His name. He had made them an elect people, that they might be the interpreters, custodians, and witnesses of His name. When they dishonored it in their own land and degraded it among the Gentiles, He redeemed and restored them for the sanctification of His name. "I do not this for your sakes, but for Mine holy name's sake, which ye have profaned among the heathen, whither ye went. And I will sanctify My great name."

Our Lord speaks in terms of Deity. To pray in Christ's name means something more than adding "for Christ's sake" to our petitions. The name expresses personality, character, and essence. The person is in the name. Prayer in Christ's name is prayer according to the quality of His person, according to the character of His mind, and according to the purpose of His will. To pray in the name of Christ is to pray as one who is at one with Christ, whose mind is the mind of Christ, whose desires are the desires of Christ, and whose purpose is one with that of Christ.

Such correspondence and identification with Christ secure the balance and interpretations of the promises given to prayer. The absolute and unconditional promises find their relativity and conditions in Him. In the Old Testament prayer was conditioned upon urgency, intensity, and sincerity. God was found of men when they cried unto Him out of a great need; when they sought Him with all their heart, and when there was sincerity of purpose and motive. Men found that God required truth in the innermost soul, and that they were not heard if they regarded iniquity in their hearts, or came to Him with insincere pretenses upon their lips. Our Lord demanded importunity and a forgiving spirit of all who prayed. In prayer in Christ's name all conditions are unified and simplified in Him. Sincerity is tested in the name. Motive is judged in the name. Prayer is proved in the name. Prayer is sanctified in the name. Prayer is endorsed by the name, when it is in harmony with the character, mind, desire, and purpose of the name. That is why in John 15:7 the words of Christ are interchangeable with His name. "If ye abide in Me, and My words abide in you, ye shall ask what ye will, and it shall be done unto you." It is something like the word of the Psalmist: "Delight thyself also in the Lord; and He shall give thee the desires of thine heart"; or that of John: "Beloved, if our heart condemn us not, then have we confidence toward God. And whatsoever we ask, we receive of Him, because we keep His commandments, and do those things that are pleasing in His sight" (1 John 3:21–22). Prayers offered in the name of Christ are scrutinized and sanctified by His nature, His purpose, and His will. They are endorsed by Him.

"For the Sake of the Name"

It means more than that. We are heard for His sake. He is the petitioner. He ever liveth to make intercession for us. In the Apocalypse He is represented as taking our prayers and adding to them the fire of the altar that makes them prevail. He told His disciples He was going to the Father, and that He was going to pray on their behalf, and whatever they asked of the Father in His name the Father would do it. Not for their own sake, but for His sake they would be heard.

When I was in Leeds a man came a long way to look over some works in which he was interested. He had written to the firm, but his request was politely declined. He went to the works and presented his card. It was returned, and he was refused. No argument could get him beyond the little shutter in the outer office. He told his disappointment to a friend, who suggested I might be able to help him. He came to see me. I gave him my card, and wrote to the head of the firm. The next day he presented his request and handed in my card, and immediately every door opened to him. His petition was granted, but not for his own sake. The head of the firm saw me in him.

In some such way we pray in Christ's name. He endorses our petitions and makes our prayers His own, and "the Father hears Him pray." We are not heard for our much speaking, not for our loud shouting. Neither are we heard for our fine phrasing, nor our much weeping. Neither are we heard for our good works, nor for our self-denials. Prayer in His name is heard for His name's sake. In the secret sanctuary of the inner chamber we ask, seek, and knock in His holy name, and present our prayers in the sure confidence of His wonderful and glorious word: "Ye did not choose Me, but I chose you, and appointed you . . . that whatsoever ye shall ask of the Father in My name, He may give it you."

"Ask, and ye shall receive."

7

Praying in the Spirit

ARLY in the year 1882 there came to me an experience that lifted my life to a new plane of understanding and of power. I received the gift of the Holy Spirit. I was led in ways I did not know, for I had hardly so much as heard that such an experience was possible. The demands of an impossible task awakened me to a sense of need. I had neither power nor might in either service or prayer. I began to pray for power for service, and God led me to the answer by way of equipment for prayer. It was a great surprise to me, for I thought I knew how to pray and had prayed much over the work to which He had sent me.

When I began to seek power, my ears were opened before my eyes began to see. I heard testimonies to which I had been deaf. Others had been driven to God baffled by lack of power, but they always associated the gift of power with an experience of holiness—about which I was not keen. It was power I wanted. I wanted power that I might succeed, and my chief concern for power was the success it would bring. I wanted success that would fill the chapel, save the people, and bring

· 57 ·

down the strong fortifications of Satan with a crash. I
was young, and I was in a hurry. Twelve of us began
to pray in band, and the answer came by

> "A way no more expected,
>   Than when His sheep
>   Passed through the deep,
> By crystal walls protected."

He led us to Pentecost. The key to all my life is in that
experience. It awakened my mind as well as cleansed
my heart. It gave me a new joy and a new power, a
new love and a new compassion. It gave me a new
Bible and a new message. Above all else, it gave me a
new understanding and a new intimacy in the
communion and ministry of prayer; it taught me to
pray in the Spirit.

The Co-operation of the Spirit

The work of the Holy Spirit is always in co-
operation. He never works alone. He depends upon
human co-operation for the mediation of His mind,
the manifestation of His truth, and the effectual
working of His will. He indwells the Body of Christ, as
Christ dwelt in the body prepared for Him by the Holy
Spirit. Revelation came from the Spirit of Truth as
men of God were inspired by Him. The word is His,
but the writing is with the hands of men. This two-
fold action runs through the whole of redemption by
Christ Jesus. Our Lord was born of a woman but was
conceived by the Holy Spirit of God. He grew in
stature and in knowledge in the house of Joseph,
instructed and guided by the Holy Spirit. His teaching

and ministry were in the power of the same Spirit. He offered Himself without blemish unto God through the eternal Spirit, and it was the Spirit that raised up Christ from the dead. There is the same co-operation in all the experience of salvation. There is always a human and divine factor. There is a two-fold witness, a two-fold leading, a two-fold work, and a two-fold intercession. We pray in the Spirit, and the Spirit maketh intercession for us.

The Fellowship of the Spirit in Prayer

The Holy Spirit does nothing of Himself, neither does He do anything for Himself. His mission is to glorify Christ, and all He does is based upon the finished work of Christ. He could not be given until Jesus was glorified, and in experience there can be no Pentecost until there is a Coronation. The Spirit is the Coronation gift of Jesus, whom the Father has made to be both Lord and Christ. The fellowship of the Spirit in prayer is made possible by an experience in Christ. The sequence is set forth in the eighth chapter of Romans (verses 9 to 27). Those who pray in the Spirit must be in the Spirit, and if the Spirit of God is to make intercession for us He must dwell in us. If we live after the flesh, we die; if we are led by the Spirit, and walk not after the flesh but after the Spirit, then the Spirit dwells in us, lives through us, and works by us. Then comes to pass that which it written: "And in like manner the Spirit also helpeth our infirmities: for we know not how to pray as we ought; but the Spirit Himself [that dwelleth in us] maketh intercession for

us with groanings which cannot be uttered; and He
that searcheth the hearts knoweth what is the mind of
the Spirit, because He maketh intercession for the
saints according to the will of God." The Holy Spirit
searches the deep things of God: He takes of the things
of Christ and reveals them unto us. God knows the
mind of the Spirit; we pray in the Spirit, instructed
and inspired by Him, and He makes intercession for
us in wordless intercession. That is the New Testament
explanation of prayer that prevails. Though I did not
know it until years after, that is what happened to me
when God gave me a new understanding, a new joy,
and a new power in prayer. A new Personality entered
a new temple, and set up a new altar. As I live, yet not
I; so I pray, yet not I. I pray in the Spirit, and the
Spirit Himself also maketh intercession. The Spirit in
my spirit prays.

The Spirit Helping Our Infirmities

He instructs and inspires all true prayer. There is
no truer word than that "we know not what we should
pray for as we ought." There is no realm in which we
so soon come to the end of what we know as in that of
prayer. Our petitions urge wants that are immediate,
obvious, and urgent. We cannot see deep enough or
far enough to know what is our real need. Most people
would like good health, home comfort, congenial
conditions, happy friendships, a little more money, and
better success; but who can tell if these would be for
their ultimate good? God sees deeper and farther, and
He may will otherwise. How often have people who

have pleaded with breaking hearts that a life might be spared lived to thank God that the Lord took when He did? He knew what was coming, and took them from the evil to come. The Holy Spirit knows the mind of Christ and the will of God, and He teaches us how to pray and what to pray for. If any man lack wisdom, let him ask of God, and He will give him more than wisdom, He will give Him the Spirit of Wisdom to instruct, strengthen, and guide.

The Holy Spirit creates the conditions of prayer. We may ask amiss, not only in what we ask but also in the reason for asking. He sanctifies desire and directs it into the will of God so that we desire what God wills to give. That is how it comes to pass that if we delight ourselves in the Lord, we can be sure that He will give us the desires of our heart. We want what He wills. The Spirit brings to expression the unutterable things of the soul. His groanings are before our praying, and our prayers are born of His travail. In Him is the supply of life and desire, wisdom and faith, intercession and power. He quickens desire, purifies motive, inspires confidence, and assures faith.

The Prayer of the Spirit

This is the inner meaning of prayer. It is more than asking, it is communion, fellowship, co-operation, identification, with God the Father and the Son by the Holy Spirit. Prayer is more than words, for it is mightiest when wordless. It is more than asking, for it reaches its highest glory when it adores and asks nothing. When a child entered his father's study and walked up to him at his desk, the father turned and asked, "What do you want, Sonnie?" The little chap answered, "Nothing, Daddy, I just came to be with you."

This mystery of the Spirit is the key to other mysteries. The secret of the Lord is made manifest to those who pray in the fellowship of the Spirit. There are stages of prayer. In one stage we pray and ask Him to help. There is a more wonderful way in which He prays and we assent, and His praying is ours. He makes intercession within the temple of our hearts, and our Lord ever lives to make intercession for us at the right hand of the Father. The Spirit within our spirit prays, working in us to will and to do the will and good pleasure of our Father who is in heaven. He is God the Spirit representing God the Father and God the Son, and the Three are one God. He is the power that worketh in us. He it is that unifies hearts in prayer and makes them an irresistible unity in intercession. The assurance of answered prayer comes from Him, and He it is that makes prayer the mightiest force in the universe of God. The secret of it all is in Him. The power of it all is by Him. The joy of it all is with Him. The biggest thing God ever did for me was to teach me to pray in the Spirit.

"We are never really men of prayer in the best sense, until we are filled with the Holy Ghost."

Therefore, Lord, teach us to pray in the Spirit!

8

Praying to God Our Father

OUR LORD bases prayer on personal relationship. He taught us to call God our Father, and the implication of sonship changes the whole aspect of prayer. Whatever difficulties may remain, intercourse must be possible between father and child, and to suggest that a child may not ask of a father would be to empty the terms of all meaning. It is a child's right to ask, and it is a father's responsibility to hear in affectionate sympathy and discerning love. The wonder is not that God hears prayer, but that He is our Father. The greater wonder includes the less. The revelation that God is Father establishes the possibility and reasonableness of prayer. The one establishes the other. God would not be Father if His children could not pray. All the teaching of Jesus about the supremacy of the child-heart in the Kingdom of God is rank blasphemy if God is not our Father. The relationship carries with it accessibility, intimacy, and fearless love. Sons of great men have sometimes remembered their father as an institution rather than as a father, and God is to some of His children little more than an institution. It was not thus that Jesus revealed Him.

Our Father in Heaven

There is no lowering of His majesty in the intimacy of the family relationship. He is still the Holy and Most High God; the High and Lofty One, that inhabiteth eternity. The Sermon on the Mount, with its relation of God to sparrows and lilies, detracts nothing from the majesty of Isaiah's vision of Him: "The everlasting God, the Lord, the Creator of the ends of the earth." He is still "the King eternal, immortal, invisible, the only wise God ... the Blessed and Only Potentate, the King of Kings, and Lord of Lords, who only hath immortality, dwelling in the light which no man can approach; whom no man hath seen, nor can see" (1 Tim. 1:17; 6:15–16).

There are many such revelations of the Divine Glory and Majesty, and it is well to ponder them in adoring worship; but Jesus Christ turned them into terms of filial virtue. He is our value. He is our Father! That is the crowning fact. To the child He is just Father. Others may cringe in fear, but the child-heart is a stranger to terror. I have never forgotten the dread that gripped me when, as a youth, I was invited to go for an interview at the manse. I walked past the door several times before I had courage to ring the bell, and as I stood at the door my heart throbbed in my ears. Imagine my surprise, when shown into the room, to find the great man on all fours, giving a ride to riotously happy children who turned his long beard into driving reins! He was their father! They knew nothing of the awe in which others stood of him, and as they grew older and knew something of his greatness their reverence deepened, but their fearlessness was not diminished. The children of the house are free and fearless.

"Pray to Thy Father Which Is in Secret"

The heavens cannot contain God our Father, but He dwells in the inner chamber of the soul. He is in secret, and seeth in secret. He waits and watches for the opening of the sanctuary door. It is holy ground, and must be approached with reverence. The soul must summon all its powers for this its holiest exercise. Here the mind must be at its best, that it may think of God and life. Thought of God is more than thinking of our thoughts about Him. Communion is deeper than theology. Prayer in secret is life finding expression in the realized Presence of God our Father. All things are voluntarily laid bare before Him. All pretense is stripped from motive, all hypocrisy from desire, all dissimulation from speech. A season of silence is the best preparation for speech with God. Infinite glory finds new value when interpreted in terms of Fatherhood, and prayer finds new horizons in the majesty of our Father in heaven.

If God be Father we may pray, but if He is such a Father why need we pray?

"When ye pray, use not vain repetitions, as the heathen do: for they think that they shall be heard for their much speaking. Be not ye therefore like unto them: for your Father knoweth what things ye have need of, before ye ask Him" (Matt. 6:7–8). Then what need is there to ask? We do not pray to inform God. Neither do we pray to persuade Him, for His love needs neither to be induced nor coaxed. No father answers his son's prayer for bread with a stone, or the request for a fish with a scorpion. Wisdom and love combine to answer need, and not to make sport of infirmity. Our earthly fathers, notwithstanding their evil natures, know better than to mock the needs and trust of their children. "If ye then, being evil, know how to give good gifts unto your children, how much more shall your Father which is in heaven give good things to them that ask Him? Ask, and it shall be given you; seek, and ye shall find; knock, and it shall be opened unto you. For every one that asketh, receiveth; and he that seeketh, findeth; and to him that knocketh, it shall be opened" (Matt. 7:11,7–8).

"If Ye Call on Him as Father"

It is no part of our purpose to discuss the problems of prayer. We are seeking to learn how to pray, and barren speculations have nothing to teach us. No part of the man must be shut out when the man is shut in. Reason is as truly of God as emotion, and either divorced from the other leaves the soul maimed and incapacitated. Vision comes to love apart from reason, but reason conserves the vision and translates it into life. Our spiritual life stands in knowledge of God, but it is not a knowledge that is acquired or achieved by the energy of flesh and blood. Love is the bond of fellowship in prayer. Attempts to rationalize love damp its fires, but where reason is dethroned, emotion becomes a conflagration. The study and the oratory are allies, but the inner chamber is better to be a place apart; then prayer enlightens thinking, and thinking kindles the altar fires of the heart. God as Father is the key to the problem of prayer. God is more than a Creator. He is our Father: heavenly Father, holy Father, righteous Father; the God of Love and still the God of Law. "The Sabbath was made for man," and the universe of God was made for the family of God.

"In the Glory of His Father"

The fact that we pray to God our Father in heaven tells us much as to how we should pray. The Son of God gloried in the glory of His Father. It was His habit to rise early that He might behold His glory and delight in His presence. He rejoiced in the Father's greatness and in the majesty of His power. It is good to go over His affirmations of the Father. "MY FATHER!" The accents of adoring love vibrate in every tone. "God is spirit; and they that worship Him must worship Him in spirit and in truth, for the Father seeketh such to worship Him." "My Father . . . is greater than all. . . . I and the Father are one."

He loved to dwell upon the care and bounty of the Father's love. Nothing is insignificant. Each is to the Infinite as if there were no other. Even the odd sparrow is not forgotten, and man is so much the more the child of His care that even the hairs of his head are numbered. He lived in the sovereign will of the

Holy and Righteous Father. He did not pray to subdue the Father's will to His desire; but that the will of the Father might be done. The sweat and agony of prayer were in the strong praying of the Father's Son, and it was always in obedience to the Father's will.

Because we pray to our heavenly Father in the secret place of prayer, we may pray with the artless unreserve of little children. There is nothing about which we may not pray. We pray as His children, and we trust Him as our heavenly Father. His answer will transcend our asking. Prayer is in itself a discipline and an education. The Spirit instructs and trains in the school of prayer. A true father waits to bless in discretion, as well as in readiness. Sometimes He waits for us. Sometimes the answer is given long before the one who prayed is told, but "every one that asketh, receiveth." Dr. Adoniram Judson, as he lay dying, heard of the remarkable answer to his prayer for the Jews when he was a missionary in Burma, and he uttered this testimony: "I never prayed sincerely and earnestly for anything but it came; at some time—no matter how distant the day—somehow, in some shape, probably the last I should have devised, it came."

"When thou prayest, enter into thy inner chamber, and when thou hast shut thy door, pray to thy Father which is in secret"—

"UNTO HIM THAT IS ABLE TO DO EXCEEDING ABUNDANTLY ABOVE ALL THAT WE ASK OR THINK."

9

The Importunity of Prayer

OUR LORD taught men to pray to God as Father. That is the central fact of His teaching. "When ye pray say, Our Father, which art in heaven." He rebukes all parade and pretense in prayer. It must be in the secret place, and the door must be shut. Within the secret place there must be simplicity and sincerity. Hypocrisy cannot live where either much speaking or fine phrasing is forbidden. Fathers and children do not make speeches to each other. God is not far off. He is near. He does not need to be informed, for Jesus says, "For your Father knoweth what things ye have need of before ye ask Him." Neither does He need to be persuaded; "for if ye, being evil, know how to give good gifts unto your children, how much more shall your Father which is in heaven give good things to them that ask Him?" Nothing could be simpler, more natural, more assuring. "Ask, and ye shall receive; for every one that asketh receiveth."

Importunity and Persistence

Alongside this teaching there come the parables of the Friend at Midnight and the Unjust Judge. They are not like His other parables, for they teach by contrast and not by comparison. God is not like the reluctant friend or the unjust judge. Then why tell the stories? The point in common between them and prayer is that in both *importunity prevails*. If the suppliants were not heard for their much speaking, their persistence had much to do with their prevailing. What place is there for such importunity in the prayers of children to their heavenly Father?

Our Lord Himself prayed with intensity and importunity. He rose early to pray. He spent all nights in prayer. The Epistle to the Hebrews (5:7) tells us that He offered up prayers and supplications with strong crying and tears. The awe of Gethsemane is full of mystery. He called upon God as Father, but in His praying there was the sweat and agony of blood. "He kneeled down and prayed, saying, Father, if Thou be willing, remove this cup from Me: nevertheless not My will, but Thine, be done . . . and being in an agony He prayed more earnestly; and His sweat became as it were great drops of blood falling down to the ground" (Luke 22:41–44). St. Matthew (26:38–46) tells us that He prayed a third time using the same words. He wrought many mighty works in nature and in men, calming the tempest, casting out demons and raising the dead, but in none of them is there any trace of strain or travail. Virtue went out of Him and He wearied in toil, but there was the ease of mastery in all

He did; but of His praying it is said, "As He prayed He sweat." He prayed in agony unto blood. If God be Father, why such agony in the praying of His Son?

"Prayer and Supplication"

There is a group of words that greatly enlarge the scope of asking and modify the impression of ease and simplicity of prayer. The man at midnight was prepared to make supplication and entreat with importunity till his request was granted. That is not much like praying to a heavenly Father. God is not like that, but praying that prevails *is* like that. The same is true of the parable of the Unjust Judge. God is not like him, but prayer pleads and persists until it prevails. Petition asks, supplication entreats, pleading argues. Job asks for an opportunity to plead his cause: "Oh that I knew where I might find Him, that I might come even to His seat! I would order my cause before Him, and fill my mouth with arguments. I would know the words which He would answer me, and understand what He would say unto me" (Job 23:3–5). God invites to reason, and prayer is given the right to plead, but if God be Father, knowing what we need, waiting to be asked, why should there be supplication and pleading?

Striving and Wrestling

When Peter was in prison "prayer was made without ceasing of the Church unto God for him" (Acts 12:5). The Revised Version substitutes "earnestly" for "without ceasing." They continued earnestly in prayer.

They prayed all night, and kept on praying until the answer came. There was the same contending in the prayer of the Syro-Phoenician woman. She came to grips and held on until Jesus commended her faith and granted her request. Striving is a family word in the New Testament. St. Paul exhorts the Christians in Rome "by our Lord Jesus Christ, and by the love of the Spirit, that ye strive together with me in your prayers to God for me" (Rom. 15:30). He commends Epaphras as a praying pastor who strove and labored in prayer (Col. 4:12), and tells the Colossians how greatly he himself strove for them. Prayer is work that involves contending, a toil that implies labor; but why should it be a toil and a labor?

Even the idea of wrestling is associated with prayer. It is not suggested that we wrestle with God, but there is a grip and grappling that calls for vigilance and concentration. It is quite clear that prayer is not the easy thing that seems to be implied in the simplicity of asking our heavenly Father for what we want and getting it. There is travail in it. There is work in it. There is entreaty in it. There is importunity in it. Maybe Coleridge was not far wrong when he spoke of prayer as the highest energy of which the human heart is capable and the greatest achievement of the Christian's warfare on earth.

The Paradox of Prayer

Prayer is full of apparent contradictions. It is so simple that a child can pray, and it is so profound that the wisest cannot explain its mystery. It is so easy that those who have no strength can pray, and it is so strenuous that it taxes every resource of energy, intelligence, and power. It is so natural that it need not be taught, and it is so far beyond nature that it cannot be learned in the school of this world's wisdom. Prayer is a world in itself, and no one aspect of life's similes can explain it. The relation of Father and child has bigger meanings in revealed truth than in our modern conception. Jesus spoke of Him as the heavenly, the holy, and the righteous Father. St. Peter combined in Him both Father and Judge. The modern mind resents prayer that is an agony and entreaty, a pleading and striving, a wrestling and persistence. That is not the way parents would like to see their children come to them, and so they reason it is not the way for them to pray.

For many years I kept by me a "check on the Bank of Heaven." It was sent to me one Christmas from America by Dr. A. T. Pierson. It was made payable to bearer, and promised to deliver on demand whatever I might need. On the face of it was the text, "My God shall supply all your need, according to His riches in glory by Christ Jesus our Lord." Prayer is just cashing checks! Is it as simple as that? Is God at the counter waiting to hand over whatever we ask? Experience soon disillusions those who think that is the whole of prayer. If that were all, why should there be a secret place and a closed door?

The Cost of Prayer

Fatherhood implies sonship, and sonship involves

correspondence of nature, character, and mind. The Holy Father is the Father of holy sons. He is in secret, and we are in secret. To be shut in alone with God is to be at the Judgment Seat. "If I regard iniquity in my heart," said the Psalmist, "the Lord will not hear me." We cannot pray as long as our hearts condemn us. God does not automatically fill orders any more than He takes them. He talks with His children and encourages them to reason with Him. He waits to bless, not only in readiness but with discretion. Prayer is a discipline and an education. Jesus spoke divine wisdom when He forbade us to cast pearls before swine: it is contrary to the Divine Order.

Intensity is a law of prayer. God is found by those who seek Him with all their heart. Wrestling prayer prevails. The fervent effectual prayer of the righteous is of great force. God hates strange fire. We must never try to work up an emotion of intensity. Avoid all that is mechanical and perfunctory. Shun the casual and flippant. Suspect all easy and cheap methods like that of the bank and the store. Leave all directors and prompters to the place of corporate and liturgical prayer. When alone with God, be alone with Him. Begin in silence. Speak with simplicity. Listen in meekness. Never leave without a conscious season of real communion. We have not to persuade God, but He has to discipline and prepare us. In all moods and at all seasons pour out the soul in prayer and supplication with thanksgiving, and if the Spirit groans in intercession do not be afraid of the agony of prayer. There are blessings of the Kingdom that are only yielded to the violence of the vehement soul.

A minister told of his Sunday School teacher who despaired of his class and asked to be released. The Superintendent persuaded him to try again, and to promise that every day for three months he would pray in secret, for every boy. Every boy in the class was saved, and four of them became ministers of great usefulness and power.

10

The Recompense of Prayer

"THY FATHER which seeth in secret shall recompense thee." Our Lord did not hesitate to associate recompense with prayer, and who can measure the blessings that come through the avenue of prayer? Those who deny that prayer changes things, or effects any wonders of deliverance and help, are among the first to exalt its influence upon the soul that prays. The value of a daily habit of withdrawal and hallowed seclusion is beyond exaggeration. The contemplation of the unseen, the attempt to think in terms of the eternal, and the honest endeavor of the soul to enter in communion with God in themselves redeem life from all that is fitful, fretful and futile. Apart altogether from specific blessings, the sheer influence of a daily habit of private prayer is incalculable. I propose to consider three, maybe four, examples.

It has been said that the mountains of the Bible well repay the climber, and no life is richer in mountain scenes than that of Moses. For forty years he had wandered among their solitary heights, feeding his flock and grappling with the great problems of his people and their God. He had been schooled in all the learning of the Egyptians, but when God wanted to instruct him He took him from the valleys and up onto a mountain. It was amid the silence of the everlasting hills that the polished courtier and distinguished scholar was fitted for the work of delivering and guiding the people of God. His service both began and ended on mountain peaks. On the eve of every new development, and on every critical occasion, God called him and he went up. Whenever the burden of his charge oppressed him, he hastened to seek God on the Mount. What he found in those ascents is still the wonder of the world.

The Mount of God was a privileged place of peculiar sanctity. God had commanded that it should be fenced, lest the cattle should trample it. "Set bounds about the mount and sanctify it." The people were not permitted to approach. Even priests and elders must stop at the boundary. No companionship was allowed. The most trusted and intimate had to be left to tarry while the servant of God went alone into the Holy Place. The Lord commanded him to get ready and come up early in the morning. God wants man at his best. All these instructions of the Pentateuch anticipate the Sermon on the Mount. There is a very special sense in which God dwells in the secret place. He is in secret: He seeth in secret. God wants us on the Mount: Come away! Come up! Come up early! Before daybreak Jesus and Moses were alone with God. Let us go up with Moses, that we may learn what he found on the Mount of God.

The Place of Revelation

MOSES FOUND GOD ON THE MOUNT

Read the story in the third chapter of Exodus. After forty years of exile for his championship of God's people, the Shepherd-Prince found the God of Israel. He was not a stranger to Him in Egypt. He had renounced the privileges and pleasures of a royal palace and cast in his lot with the afflicted people of his race. He had given proof of his zeal for the Most High, but he had never had a personal revelation of Him till he found Him that day on the Mount. There is much outer-court service in the Lord's Temple. Many serve and suffer for Him who never enter the Holy Place where the Most High dwells between the cherubim. It is there He reveals Himself as nowhere else. He manifests Himself to those who pray in secret as He cannot to those who have no inner sanctuary of the soul.

MOSES FOUND HIMSELF WHERE HE FOUND HIS GOD

It was not a pleasant discovery; it seldom is. He was a disappointed reformer. He had made great sacrifices for Israel, and he found them resentful of his interference, jealous of his motives, distrustful of his purpose. For forty years he had brooded over a wicked king, a spiritless and ungrateful people. He nursed his grievance with the resignation of a martyr and the despondency of a disappointed leader. "Put thy hand in thy bosom," commanded the Voice out of the Fire; and, lo, it was leprous, white as snow! That was a startling surprise for him. He had thought the other people were leprous, but neither his own heart nor hands were clean. That is the kind of discovery men make on the Mount of God, and that is one reason we are so reluctant to ascend. He discovered other things besides leprosy. He found himself. He found latent powers. He found his vocation. He found that a stick he had carried daily was a symbol and instrument of divine power. God discovers us to ourselves when He reveals Himself to us.

MOSES FOUND THE WILL OF GOD ON THE MOUNT

It was there he received the law. After forty days alone with God he brought Heaven's laws to earth on two tablets of stone. Those laws remain to this day the foundation of all righteous government among men. After centuries of progress they are still the basis of civilization.

He not only received the Commandments which were to be the cornerstones of good government for all time; he also received directions concerning local and personal details. See the minute instructions for the building of the Tabernacle. No trifle is overlooked. Nails and fringes, tongs and snuffers are all included. Every detail was designed on the Mount. Every pattern was divinely fixed and approved. The way to the Mount is still open. The divine pattern of each life is still to be seen in the secret place of the Most High God. The humblest follower of Jesus may know the divine will at first hand. It is every man's privilege to be fully assured in the will of God. The divine attention to detail is amazing. Nothing is too trivial for

Omniscience. Come straight to God. Do not bother other people. Lay all questions naked before Him, and He will make it plain to you what is His will. When God speaks, His speech is easily understood. All questions of the plain should be settled on the Mount, and where there is certainty on the Mount there will be victory on the levels and in the valleys.

The Place of Power

There is a wonderful story in Exodus 17. It was Israel's first battle. The Amalekites came against them in Rephidim. Joshua commanded the hosts of Israel, and Moses went up onto the Mount to pray. The fluctuations of the battle were astonishing. In turn the opposing hosts prevailed, until it was found that the issue of the battle was not with the fighters in the field but with the intercessors on the Mount. It was the weaponless hand of prayer that ruled the battle. "And it came to pass, when Moses held up his hand, that Israel prevailed: and when he let down his hand, Amalek prevailed." Is it necessary to point out the moral of the tale? Power is the recompense of prayer. It takes us long to learn that prayer is more important than organization, more powerful than armies, more influential than wealth, and mightier than all learning. Prevailing prayer makes men invincible. They who prevail in the secret place of the Most High cannot be beaten anywhere. All things are possible to secret prayer.

The Place of Fellowship

On the Mount the Lord spoke unto Moses face to face, as a man speaketh unto his friend. Like Abraham, Moses was admitted to the friendship of God. He did not come simply to plead petitions and receive orders. He was there for communion on a common basis of fellowship. The inner chamber is an audience chamber where the soul enters into friendly intercourse and mutual interchange. It is a place for listening as well as for speech. The most important part of prayer is not what we say to God but what God says to us. It is no place for hurry. The soul must be still and wait before the Lord.

The Mount is the place of intercession. There is a moving story in Exodus 32:9–14 of how Moses pleaded for Israel. He stepped into the breach. God looks for men who will stand in the gap (Ezek. 22:30). God encourages us to speak for others and to plead for them. He suffers entreaty. How daring was Abraham's faith! With what audacity Moses stepped into the breach and urged the plea for Israel! With what passion Paul pleaded for his kinsmen according to the flesh! We are commanded to pray one for another, and who can tell what blessings come to men through intercession?

It was on the Mount Moses saw God's glory. It is a vision of the secret place. It was on the Mount Jesus was transfigured. The glory seen is also shared. Prayer transfigures. Moses came down from the Mount all aglow with the glory, but "he wist not that the skin of his face shone." That is the secret of radiant humility.

"As Jesus prayed, He was transfigured before them." Glory is the recompense of prayer. The Lord who calls His servant onto the Mount sends him down. Peter wanted to stay. We go up that we may go down. We enter in that we may come out. There are golden images, senseless and wicked passions, enslaved and misguided people, distracted fathers and demon-torn sons and daughters that need the vision and the power of God. Come up! Go down! God wants us on the Mount and He wants us in the valley. Moses died on the Mount. Those who go up and down at God's bidding are sure to end in going up to come down no more.

11

The Power of Prayer

ELIJAH is chosen in the New Testament as the example of prayer. There were many others in the Old Testament Scriptures who prayed and prevailed, for they abound with stories of those who called upon God and were mightily delivered. Jacob so prayed that his name was changed from Jacob to Israel. Moses was preeminently a man of prayer; he was sustained, guided, and transformed by prayer. Daniel prayed habitually and continually, and his life was a romance of prayer. There were others, from Abraham to the last of the Old Testament prophets, including kings and priests, soldiers and reformers, widows and sufferers. Why was Elijah chosen among them all?

A Mighty Man

Elijah occupies a larger place in the New Testament than in the Old, and it is always an advantage when the New Testament gives the interpretation of an Old Testament theme. The Old Testament story offers no explanation of the prophet's power. His ministry consisted in a series of dramatic appearances, and the most sensational event in a sensational life was its dramatic end. For the most part he dwelt in solitary places, and he was always a solitary figure. "I alone" was a plaint often on his lips. The Old Testament closes with a promise of his return, and the New Testament opens with the record of its fulfillment. He championed God, defied kings, and held the destiny of nations in his hand.

The New Testament explanation of the man and his work is that he was a man of prayer. On the face of the Old Testament story, prayer was an outstanding feature of this man, but according to the New Testament, prayer was the entire explanation of the man and his marvelous doings. That he was a mountain of a man is plain for all men to see, but he was a man of like passions with other men, and whatever difference there was between him and others was due to prayer. St. James says, "Elijah was a man of like passions with us, and he prayed"—that is what made him different. Prayer accounts for the man, as it accounts for Abraham and Jacob, David and Daniel, but there was something in Elijah's praying that gave distinction even among saints mighty in prayer. What was it? Why did Jehovah come to be known as the Lord God of Elijah?

Miracles of Power

The praying of Elijah is a demonstration of the supernatural power of prayer. His prayers were miracles of power. That is what the New Testament says of them. There has always been difficulty with the translation of James 5:16. The Authorized Version reads:

"The effectual fervent prayer of a righteous man availeth much."

The Revised Version:
"The supplication of a righteous man availeth much in its working."

Dr. Rendel Harris translates it:
"The energized prayer of a righteous man is of great force."

Prayer with Elijah was force, supernatural power, miraculous in its working. He never discussed natural law and he never doubted supernatural power. He prayed and there was no rain, and when he prayed for rain it came in floods. He prayed for life to come again to the dead child of the widow with whom he lodged, and the soul of the child returned. He prayed for fire from heaven, and it fell as he prayed. He did not argue about prayer. He prayed. Praying solves problems of prayer.

There always have been problems about prayer. In the wilderness they questioned God's power to transcend known laws of His world. "Can God . . . ?" The answer of faith turns the question into an affirmation and believes God can. These are hardly the days in which it is safe to say that anything is impossible. We stand on the threshold of unexplored worlds, and if so much that was incredible has become possible to man, who shall say that anything is impossible to God? If the thought of man can be spoken and heard thousands of miles away, who dares put limits to the thoughts and purpose of God? He who made the heavens and earth must be bigger than His worlds, and it is impossible He should be imprisoned within His own laws. The prayer of faith links man's petition to the power of God. All men believe in the power of prayer to influence mind, develop character, and sanctify motive and will, but that is not all. Prayer is force. Prayer changes things. The Lord God of Elijah had sovereign and omnipotent power, and these were at the command of the prayer of faith. Every praying man knows of answers to prayer to which there is no explanation but in God. I am reluctant to quote examples, but in my own life they abound, and the language of Psalm 116 is often on my lips:

> " I love the Lord, because He hath heard
> My voice and my supplications.
> Because He hath inclined His ear unto me,
> Therefore will I call upon Him as long as I live."

There is one remarkable instance that I cherish because of the way the story came to me. There are two buildings in the city of Bristol which are monuments of answered prayer. One is Müller's orphanage, and of the other I am not at present at liberty to speak. Dr. A. T. Pierson was my friend, and he was the friend and biographer of Müller. It was from him I got the first half of the story. He told me of an occasion when he was the guest of Müller at the orphanage. One night when all the household had retired he asked Pierson to join him in prayer. He told him that there was absolutely nothing in the house for the next morning's breakfast. My friend tried to remonstrate with him and to remind him that all the stores were closed. Müller knew all that. He had prayed as he always prayed, and he never told anyone of his needs but God. They prayed. At least Müller did, and Pierson tried to. They went to bed and slept, and breakfast for two thousand children was there in abundance at the usual breakfast hour. Neither Müller nor Pierson ever knew how the answer came. The story was told next morning to Simon Short of Bristol, under pledge of secrecy till the benefactor died. The details of it are thrilling, but all that need be told here is that the Lord called him out of bed in the middle of the night to send breakfast to Müller's orphanage, and knowing nothing of the need or of the two men at prayer, he sent provisions that would feed them for a month. That is like the Lord God of Elijah, and still more like the God and Father of our Lord Jesus Christ.

The Greatest Force on Earth

It is not every kind of praying that works such wonders. It takes a man of prayer to pray as Elijah and George Müller prayed. It is the energized prayer of the righteous man that is of great force. The widow knew that Elijah was a man of God when he prayed her boy back to life (1 Kings 17:24). It is always the crowning proof and the ultimate test. Nothing would turn the nation back to God so surely and so quickly as a Church that prayed and prevailed. The world will never believe in a religion in which there is no supernatural power. A rationalized faith, a socialized Church, and a moralized gospel may gain applause, but they awaken no conviction and win no converts.

There is passion in the praying that prevails. Elijah was a man of passions all compact. There was passion in all he did. All there was of him went into everything he did. God loves a man aflame. The lukewarm He cannot abide. He never keeps hot hearts waiting. "Then will I be found of you when ye seek Me with all your hearts." When Elijah prayed, he prayed in his prayer. Is there not much praying in which there is no prayer? The praying man was in his petition. Listen to his praying in the death chamber. Watch him on Carmel. Hear him plead the honor of God and cry unto the Lord for the affliction of the people. It is always the same: Abraham pleading for Sodom, Jacob wrestling in the stillness of the night, Moses standing in the breach, Hannah intoxicated with sorrow, David heartbroken with remorse and grief—Jesus in a sweat of blood. Add to the list from the records of the Church, personal observation and experience, and always there is the cost of passion unto blood. It prevails. It turns ordinary mortals into men of power. It brings power. It brings fire. It brings rain. It brings life. It brings God. There is no power like that of prevailing prayer.

Recent correspondence has brought me many stories of answered prayer. I can quite understand why critical minds have misgivings as to their evidential value. The man who has not travailed through the supplication is always free to look for other explanations, but to the man who has prayed the explanation adds to the wonder of the answer. He had the answer before the answer came. Take one example. A man tells me of a great anxiety in his business life. Like Jehoshaphat, he had no resources to meet the need, and he knew not what to do, but he continued earnestly in prayer and supplication to God until one day there came a great peace into his soul and he knew that he was heard. The conditions were unchanged, but he had an assurance of peace, and in a most unexpected way and by a comparatively unknown person, deliverance came. The explanation was obvious, but the answer was no less sure.

It always seems to me quite useless to argue about prayer; a challenge like that made by Huxley is utterly futile. The proof that God answers prayer is in praying. I once answered a street-corner challenge to prove that God answers prayer by challenging the man to come and kneel down and pray, but the challenge was not accepted. I still hold that to be the only way, and that way is scientific and conclusive.

Another story that I may repeat comes from the Rev. T. A. Turney. He was a scholar in a school where the schoolmaster was both the master and his uncle. The man was one of the old sort, who taught by making his scholars find out things for themselves. He was harder with his nephew than with the rest, lest he should be suspected of favoritism. The lad came to a deadlock like that which awaits us all at some stage of learning. There was a problem in mathematics he could not do. Day after day he brought it to the master, only to be sent back to try again. When this had gone on for more than a week, the lad went one night to a mission service and gave his heart to God. At the communion rail he began to pray. When he got home he turned again to his problem, with the same result. So when he knelt down to pray he once more asked God to help him with this problem. In the night—asleep or awake he does not know—he saw the proposition worked out. He got up and wrote it down. Next morning he took it to the master, who answered sharply, "Right! Who showed you?"

"God," answered the boy.

An Energized Intercessor

Have you ever heard of "Praying Hyde"? The fact that John Hyde came by the universal accord of his intimates to be called "Praying Hyde" dates back to the day when he received the baptism of the Holy Spirit. In that experience his amazing prayer life began. The recorded answers to prayer are the least part of his record. He prayed the Indian Keswick into existence. He prayed thousands into the Kingdom of God and hundreds of laborers into the harvest fields of God. Above and beyond all this he prayed himself into the mystery of fellowship in our Lord's intercession. The secret of his prayer life is that it was a life of prayer.

He was in England in 1911. He went to a mission service where Wilbur Chapman and Charlie Alexander were having a hard time. He took the burden of the mission upon his heart and prayed until victory came. After a meeting of wonderful power, Dr. Chapman asked Mr. Hyde to pray for him, and this is his account of what happened:

He came to my room, turned the key in the door, dropped on his knees, waited five minutes without a single syllable coming from his lips. I could hear my own heart thumping and his beating. I felt the hot tears running down my face. I knew I was with God. Then with upturned face, down which the tears were streaming, he said: "Oh, God!" Then for five minutes at least he was still again, and then, when he knew he was talking with God, his arm went around my shoulder, and there came up from the depth of his heart such petitions for men as I had never heard before. I rose from my knees to know what real prayer was. We believe that prayer is mighty, and we believe it as we never did before.

I am aware that such records of prayer life may discourage where they were meant to inspire. I am not asking that you and I should be fashioned after the pattern of exceptional men, but I do rejoice that whatever was given to one is available for all.

12

Praying and
the Commonplace

MOSES and Elijah were not
ordinary men. They were so
unusual that they were chosen from among all the Old
Testament saints to come and talk with Jesus on the
Mount of Transfiguration. One was the Leader of the
Old Covenant, and the other was the most dramatic
of its prophets. Their tasks were unique. God called
them to duties that demanded frequent and intimate
intercourse with Himself. The miraculous was
conspicuous in all they did. The rod of Moses and the
mantle of Elijah were symbols and instruments of
power. Their prayers were miracles. They moved in
the realm of the infinite. They controlled the heavens
and commanded the earth. At their word rivers and
rain were ruled, life and death were commanded, oil
and meal multiplied. Greater than these works of
power were the results of prayer in illumination and
guidance. God revealed His mind and gave instructions as to His will. In answer to prayer there came

the revelation that was beyond human wisdom, and the miracle of the mind was greater than those of material power.

Prayer and Ordinary Folk

The dramatic stories of prevailing prayer in the Bible have made a profound impression upon the minds of ordinary people. It has standardized miracle as the normal working power of prayer. It is the true standard, for all prayer is supernatural in its working, but it has its discouraging influence. Moses stands alone, and though Elijah was a man of like passions with ourselves, he was no ordinary man and his task was by no means commonplace. What is the place and work of prayer in the life of ordinary people? What about the people in whose life there is no opportunity for either privacy or leisure, and whose duties are an unrelieved monotony of mechanical commonplace? Is prayer only for exceptional people and exceptional circumstances? Or has it a place and a work in lives of ordinary gifts and commonplace living?

Of the New Testament success of Elijah it is said that he did no miracle. He was not less a man of prayer than his Old Testament predecessor, but food did not multiply at his touch, he raised no dead, and neither water nor fire was at his command. The only miracles in him were in personality, in discernment, and in truth. So we find that supernatural power may work along normal lines of natural law. Ordinary people may pray about commonplace things, and the answer to their prayers may be in an enlightened mind, a triumphant soul, a steadfast faith, and a holy life. There may be no miraculous incidents, but prayer lifts the lowliest and most ordinary life to the exalted plane of the supernatural, and that is the greatest miracle of all.

Prayer and Daily Toil

It is quite certain that we cannot all be Elijahs or Elishas, Abrahams or Daniels, George Müllers or Hudson Taylors, Thomas Barnardos or "Praying Hydes," but that is no reason why we should not be men of prayer. There are praying men in the Scriptures of whom no miracles are told. They moved in other spheres. They were workers in the workshop of the world. Jacob and Moses were keepers of sheep, with ample spaces of solitude in which to pray. We are not told that Elijah ever worked at anything but prayer. The example of Elijah's miraculous record needs to be balanced by that of others who lived and worked among the normal conditions of life. It is expected that preachers and prophets should give themselves to the Word of God and prayer, but what about the man whose life is lived in the factory, the office, or the store? Nehemiah was as truly a man of prayer as Elijah. He was the builder of the wall of Jerusalem. He wrought no miracle, he saw no vision, he had no special commission from Heaven. He never said God had sent him, neither did he ask anyone else to say it for him. A need and an opportunity called him. That was enough. There was a condition that filled his soul with grief, a great work to be done, and no one seeming to care about it, and somehow it was laid upon him that he ought to take it in hand. So he prayed. He prayed over the evil tidings, prayed for the ruined city, prayed about the reproach of the people of God, prayed on behalf of those in distress; prayed till his heart was well nigh breaking. Nothing extraordinary happened. No angel came. God gave no sign. When Elijah prayed, things happened. Nehemiah prayed, and nothing happened! Oh, yes, there did! Something happened in *Nehemiah*, and a miracle in personality is greater than a miracle in nature. Emotion turned to prayer, and prayer turned to conviction; then conviction generated purpose, and purpose directed energy; then energy vitalized activity, until the two sayings come together:

"So I PRAYED" *and*
"So WE BUILT."

The praying of Nehemiah wrought no startling and dramatic manifestation of supernatural power, but it built the wall and restored the city, and in the will of God that was his work. Nehemiah prayed about his work. Prayer was the maintained attitude and continued habit of his life. There are those who reserve prayer for special and desperate occasions. We read of some who prayed because they were at their wits' end. Most people pray when they get there. Some pray under the stress of an emotional mood. Nehemiah prayed all the time, all the way through, and about everything. It was so entirely his habit to pray that he became a man of prayer.

The Practical Value of Prayer

The habit of prayer implies a certain attitude to life. It predicates God, and recognizes His sovereignty over all. It submits all things to His will, rehearses all things in His presence, judges all things by His standards of values, and lives by faith in Him. Prayer is the essence and test of the godly life. Who can measure its influence upon mind and character, or estimate its value in practical wisdom and dexterous skill? The Book of Nehemiah is in the Bible, and therein it is written for all to see what prayer did for the man of prayer who wrought no miracle but built the wall against tremendous odds. It gave him the commission and co-operation of the King, and secured him all necessary supplies. It brought him courage and sense in dealing with critics and adversaries, and it instructed him in wisdom in adjusting difficulties of labor and wages. It saved him from the tricky craft of the official, and gave him sagacity to resist the cunning of the enemy. It gave him sanctuary when they invented lies and slanders about him. It armed him with faith and humor as well as with a sword and trowel. He kept his hands clean, his wits alert, his courage bright, and prayed his way through. He was sure of God: sure of the character of God, the words of God, the covenant of God. So he prayed and so he trusted; so he worked and so he prevailed.

"Whatsoever Ye Shall Ask"

There is nothing about which we may not pray, but prayer will not avail if it is a mere whim or an idle wish. Nehemiah prayed over his work, but he made it his business to know all about the things of which he prayed. His work prospered because he worked at his work. It is no use to pray about work and then neglect it, or play the fool in it, for lack of courage, efficiency and sense. He prayed and used his wits. He knew the Lord would send supplies; but he took care to have the king's letters. He knew the Lord would protect; but he added a sword to the equipment of the builder's trowel. Prayer gives vision in the secret place, intelligence in work, sense in judgment, courage in temptation, tenacity in adversity, and joyous assurance in the will of God. A weaver who prayed over his work, as Nehemiah prayed over his, came to be known as the man who wove every yard of cloth for the Lord Jesus Christ. He never made a fortune, but his work prospered and his character was of rare worth. Every task and every duty may be sanctified in the Word of God and in prayer. The prayer life in which there are no miracles may be the greatest miracle of all.

The secret of life is in the secret place where God waits. Even to those to whom privacy is impossible there is a sanctuary of the soul into which they can withdraw. I want to bear my witness to the priceless value of the habit of secret prayer. There is nothing about which I do not pray. I go over all my life in the presence of God. All my problems are solved there. All questions of liberty as well as duty are settled there. I seek counsel of God, and submit all things to the judgment of God. The sanctuary of my soul is there.

There was a wonderful sight from my study window this morning. I stood and watched a gorgeous rainbow come up over the hill. It rose until it stood like a thing apart, and then it moved toward us till one end rested in the village and the other in the river. Its colors were indescribably beautiful, and it filled all the landscape with its glory. The old ruin was like a fairy palace and every cottage was a blaze of radiant beauty. The fields and the trees reflected the splendor of the heavens. Every common stick and stone was transformed into a thing of radiant beauty and holy splendor.

Even so does prayer sanctify and glorify the commonplace life of ordinary folk.

13

The Prayer of Faith

"HE THAT cometh to God must believe that He is, and that He is a rewarder of them that diligently seek Him." Faith is necessary to prayer. Without some such faith it is difficult to imagine how any man could pray. Man could not pray without faith. Therefore the faith which God demands is the first requirement in the man who prays. Atheists do not pray. God sets great store on faith. He makes it the first requisite of prayer, the sole condition of salvation, the one essential of spiritual life, and the universal law of power.

It is a shallow interpretation of faith that sneers at salvation by grace through faith alone. Faith is enough. Faith is all God asks. Faith is all Jesus asks: "Ye believe in God, believe also in Me." When the ruler of the synagogue was told that his daughter was dead, Jesus steadied his faith, saying, "Fear not: only believe"; and when the distraught father of the demoniac boy cried out against his own despair, our Lord assured him that "all things are possible to him that believeth."

Without faith it is impossible to please God. Without faith it is impossible to pray to God. Without faith it is impossible to have fellowship with God.

Without faith man can do nothing with God, and God can do nothing with man. Neither can man do anything with man apart from faith, for faith is the basis of civilization as well as of salvation.

The Law of Faith

St. Paul expounds the law of faith in relation to grace, and St. James expounds the same law in the realm of prayer. There is no controversy between them. Faith to both is more than an intellectual conviction, however sincere. It is a moral and spiritual attitude that commits the whole being to accepted and assured truth. Faith is more than belief. The demons believe and tremble, but they do not trust. Faith is trust. It is not an opinion, not a fiction, not a supposition. It is a faculty of vision, a process of verification, an assurance of knowledge, a logic of life. It demands an honest and impartial mind, a pure and disinterested motive, a loyal and steadfast obedience. This is the faith that works by law to the justification of the ungodly, the sanctification of the unholy, and to the mighty power that prevails in prayer. "For verily I say unto you, If ye have faith as a grain of mustard seed, ye shall say unto this mountain, Remove hence to yonder place; and it shall remove; and nothing shall be impossible unto you. Howbeit this kind goeth not out but by prayer and fasting" (Matt. 17:20–21). The saying in St. Matthew's Gospel must be put alongside that of St. Mark (11:22–24): "Have faith in God. For verily I say unto you, Whosoever shall say unto this mountain, Be thou taken up, and cast into the sea;

and shall not doubt in his heart, but shall believe that what he saith cometh to pass; he shall have it. Therefore I say unto you, All things whatsoever ye pray and ask for, believe that ye have received them, and ye shall have them."

The Law of Faith in Prayer

1. *Ask* (James 1:5).

The teaching of James consists chiefly of amplifications and applications of our Lord's teaching in the Sermon on the Mount. He begins where our Lord began on the subject of prayer with the simple command to ask: "If any man lack, let him ask of God." The reach of the privilege of asking covers the man's whole need as well as his lack of wisdom. God gives to all that ask, liberally and without upbraiding, therefore "Ask, and ye shall receive." There is no limit to the range of prayer. "Whatsoever" is promised to "whosoever," and the largest liberty is given to those who pray. "In nothing be anxious; but in everything by prayer and supplication with thanksgiving let your requests be made known unto God" (Phil. 4:6). "Ask, and ye shall receive" (John 16:24). Prayer is asking. "Your Father knoweth what things ye have need of, before ye ask Him. After this manner therefore pray ye" (Matt. 6:8–9). Why pray if He knows? Because asking is something different from giving information. God waits to be asked before He gives the gifts that supply man's deepest needs.

2. *Ask in Faith* (James 1:6).

Faith is explained by its opposite. Doubt is double minded and unstable. Like a troubled sea, it is driven by the force of the wind and tossed by the surge of the deep; it is at the mercy of a double motion of oscillation and undulation. Internal conditions disturb and external circumstances drive. Such a man gets nothing because he is not of one mind, and a two-minded man is unstable in all his ways.

> Ships go East and ships go West,
>   Whatever the winds that blow;
> The set of the sail, and not the gale,
>   Settles the way we go.

Faith sets the sails.

3. *Ask Aright* (James 4:3).

It is possible to ask amiss. "Ye ask, and receive not, because ye ask amiss, that ye may spend it in your pleasures." God takes account not only of what we want but of why we want it. He looks at the heart. There are some people to whom He will not give audience. Sin shuts men out. "If I regard iniquity in my heart, the Lord will not hear me" (Ps. 66:18). Unbelief shuts men out (Heb. 4:11, 11:6). An unforgiving spirit shuts men out (Matt. 5:23–24; 6:14–15; Mark 11:25–26). An unstable mind shuts men out (James 1:7). A condemning conscience shuts men out (1 John 3:21–22). A self-seeking motive shuts men out (James 4:3). Faith works in those who pray that they may ask aright.

4. *Ask Righteously* (James 5:13–18).

The rightness of the asking goes down to the rightness of the asker. The person who prays is the prayer. He is both the petitioner and the petition; the pleader and the plea; the request and the reason. Patriarchs and Psalmists fall back on their integrity as an argument with God, and their plea is admitted. The alms and prayers of Cornelius were accepted by God, and Peter declared his new faith in these terms: "Of a truth I perceive that God is no respecter of persons: but in every nation he that feareth Him and worketh righteousness is acceptable to Him" (Acts 10:34–35). It is the praying of the righteous man that is of great force. Faith is no substitute for right living. It does not cover sin; only blood can do that. It saves from sin, gives victory over sin, and makes men righteous with the righteousness of God. There is no condemnation, but an assurance in the will of God that gives "boldness toward God: and whatsoever we ask, we receive of Him, because we keep His commandments, and do those things that are pleasing in His sight" (1 John 3:21–22).

5. *Ask Earnestly.*

God promises to be found of us when we seek Him with all our hearts (Jer. 29:13). Elijah's prevailing prayer was intense in its passion. Our Lord's parables on prayer emphasize an importunity that persists and insists in spite of discouragement, and the Epistle to the Hebrews speaks of His own praying with strong cries and tears. It is the impassioned prayer that prevails.

6. *Ask in the Spirit.*

The prevailing prayer of Elijah was energized prayer. It was inspired, instructed, and empowered of the Holy Spirit.

7. *Ask in the Prayer of Faith.*

Ask believingly according to the law of faith. The principle is stated in Mark 11:24, and illustrations are throughout the Scriptures. The Honor Roll of Faith in Hebrews 11 furnishes illustrious examples of its power, and in verse 13 there is a picturesque description of its method. Like the man in the Gospels who believed the word that Jesus spoke and went his way (John 4:50), so these had witness borne to them, and they dared and endured by faith, even dying believing. Israel shouted before the walls of Jericho while as yet there was not even a crack in the solid masonry, and the shout of faith brought them down so that there was not a yard of solid masonry left. Jehoshaphat's singers chanted the song of victory before the battlefield was reached, and the song of faith was mightier than thousands of armed men skilled in war. Elijah's promise to the widow was made in the midst of famine, and in the house of faith there was no lack. The prayer of faith works mightily, for it is mighty with the power of God.

"When ye pray, believe that ye have received and ye shall have."

"HAVE FAITH IN GOD."

He never dishonors faith.

14

Praying "One for Another"

THE PRAYING people of the Bible are intercessors. Abraham pleaded for Sodom and Gomorrah. Moses made intercession for apostate Israel. Samuel prayed all night for Saul and continually for the nation. David entreated God for his people. Daniel prayed for the deliverance of the Lord's people from Babylon. Christ prayed for His disciples, and made special intercession for Peter. Paul was an example of his own exhortation "that supplications, prayers, intercessions, thanksgivings be made for all men." The one thing that is said to have surprised God is that the voice of intercession had ceased. "And He saw that there was no man, and wondered that there was no intercessor" (Isa. 59:16). His delivering mercy depends upon intercessors—people who will put their shoulders under the burdens of others. "And I sought for a man among them, that should make up the fence, and stand in the gap before Me for the land, that I should not destroy it: but I found none" (Ezek. 22:30). The normal function of prayer is to make intercession with God for others.

The Mystery of Intercession

That we may pray for others is the deepest mystery and the crowning glory of prayer. If we do not know how to pray for ourselves as we ought, how can we know how to pray for other people? If we know so imperfectly our own needs, how can we know the needs of others? Who are we that we should presume to interpret the needs of another to God? He alone knows, and may not His knowledge and love be trusted? The answer is that prayer cannot be solitary. It must be personal, but it cannot be isolated. Life is relative and interdependent, "For none of us liveth to himself" (Rom. 14:7). Prayer cannot stop at personal need. Even in the inner chamber there is no escape from the impact of those who impinge upon us in the home, the church, and the world. The law of prayer is that each stands alone in the presence of God, just as surely as "each one of us shall give account of himself to God," each bearing his own burden, and yet every man bearing the burden of others. There is always a burden. Intercession is vicarious. The Saviour made intercession because He bore the sin of the transgressors (Isa. 53:12). So it is in all prayer that entreats for others. Moses made the cause of Israel his own. (See the prayers in Exod. 17, 32, 33, 34; Num. 11, 14, 21, 27) Isaiah identified himself with the people of "unclean lips" (Isa. 6:5). Daniel made confession for the nation (Dan. 9). The despairing father of the epileptic boy (Mark 9:22) and the distracted mother of the demon-possessed daughter (Matt. 15:21–28) each made the affliction of the child a personal plea. So it has been in the history of the Christian Church. Carey bore the burden of India, Hudson Taylor of China, Livingstone of Africa; and so does everyone bear the burden of those for whom he prays.

The Intercession in Heaven

Prayer is central in heaven. The interpretation of the mystery of intercession begins there. It is fellowship in the ministry of our Great High Priest at the right hand of God. "He ever liveth to make intercession" (Heb. 7:25). That our Lord should need to pray in the days of His flesh is a mystery of humiliation; that He should need to make intercession in heaven is a mystery of glory. It is a light that transcends our vision. The "why" and the "how" are beyond our understanding, but it is because He so lives to make intercession that He is able to save to the uttermost all who come to God by Him. The truth revealed is explicit, and its effect in experience assures its certainty. The ascended Christ is the Priest-King at the right hand of God. As High Priest He represents man to God; as King He represents God to man. He entered in by the one offering of Himself as a Sacrifice for sin. Having entered by His own blood, He is the one Mediator between God and man, and humanity's advocate with the Father. He intercedes for men (Heb. 7:25, 27; 9:24). Prayer finds its expression and availableness in terms of Christ and His finished work. He takes the prayers of the earthly altar and adds to them the fires of the heavenly, and they become acceptable and effective through His name (Heb. 13:15; Rev. 5:8; 8:3). So much is revealed, and we have no authority to go beyond, but it makes clear that in the fellowship of the saints there is prayer in heaven, and there is no logic by which the redeemed can be excluded from the ministry of intercession.

The Intercession of the Spirit

There is a two-fold intercession. The High Priest intercedes for us in heaven, and the Holy Spirit intercedes within the temple of the consecrated soul. "The Spirit helpeth our infirmities: for we know not what we should pray for as we ought; but the Spirit maketh intercession for us with groanings which cannot be uttered; and He who searcheth the hearts knoweth what is the mind of the Spirit, because He maketh intercession for the saints according to the will of God" (Rom. 8:26–27). There is such unity of purpose and harmony of method in the two intercessions that the two are one, and what is prayed by the intercessor on earth is prayed by the Intercessor in heaven. The Spirit takes of the things of Christ and reveals them unto us. He takes of the deep things of God and interprets them to us. He knows the purpose of God, and makes intercession according to the divine will. In this way He works in us both to will and to do the good pleasure of His will. The unutterable groaning is in our imperfect humanity, but the inarticulate groaning of the Spirit within us finds complete expression in the terms of the heavenly priesthood.

Intercession through the Spirit implies a Spirit-filled temple. He can only interpret spiritual things to the spiritually minded, for the carnal mind cannot know the mind of the Spirit. He cannot intercede in the heart of an unyielded will. The pure in heart see God. The heart must be sensitive to light and obedient to the heavenly vision. It takes a saint to be in the ministry of intercession. There are many kinds of service that make no demand upon spirituality for their success. Preaching may be an art in which there is no power of the Spirit. The ecclesiastical ministry of outer-court stewardship may be rendered by the gifts of the office and the counter. Social service may make a fair show in official returns without any glow of spiritual-mindedness. Church music may be of a kind that does not call for the travail and anguish of intercession. The man of prayer must be a man of God.

The Intercession of the Secret Place

We are called unto the fellowship of this two-fold intercession. The terms that are used to describe it indicate sacrificial labor and sustained intensity. Nothing costs so much. St. Paul speaks of being in travail, striving and laboring in prayer. There is always the sweat of blood in prevailing intercession. The reason is not in God's reluctance, for He inspires that He may fulfill. There are many adversaries in the human will, as well as spiritual forces and personalities. God waits to bless; and that means that He is always ready and always waiting. The answer to Daniel's prayer was delayed for three weeks by some mysterious conflict in the realm of spirits (Dan. 10:12–14). "For our wrestling," says St. Paul, "is not against flesh and blood, but against the principalities, against the powers, against the world rulers of this darkness, against the spiritual hosts of wickedness in the heavenly places" (Eph. 6:12). Jesus said, "Satan hath desired to have you, that he may sift you as wheat: but I have prayed for thee" (Luke 22:31–32).

For Whom and for What May We Pray?

The general answer is, for all and for everything. The real answer is, according to the intercession of the Spirit and according to the will of God. There are those who have a natural right to our prayers, such as our families, our friends, our fellow believers, our minister and colleagues, our fellow workmen and our masters, as well as those whom we know to be in circumstances of need. The prayer of intercession calls for intelligence, understanding, watchfulness, as well as for sympathy, intensity and sacrifice. There is often a severe discipline of patience and faith. Sometimes the answer comes immediately and sometimes it tarries. The one truth in which faith rests is that it comes. The Spirit that assures is acquainted with all contingencies, and His assurances are YEA and AMEN in Christ Jesus.

I have been more mindful to set forth the sanctuary of my own faith than to give rules and to quote examples. The subject is in all the Scriptures, and its range is without boundaries. Its mysteries are unsearchable but its certainties are infallible. The blessings are immeasurable and invaluable. Who can tell the influences that have come into his life through the intercession of those who have prayed for him?

Who can measure the work of those whose ministry is that of laboring in prayer for others? The great need of God is for intercessors. "Ye that are the Lord's remembrancers, take ye no rest, and give Him no rest, till He establish, and till He make Jerusalem a praise in the earth."

He still saves by them that sigh and that cry.

15

Praying for Divine Healing

THE SUBJECT of Divine Healing is always with me. The infirmities of the flesh have kept it continually among the problems of my faith. In the work of a pastor there is no escape from it. Invalids look wistfully at the statement of the Apostle James concerning the prayer that heals the sick, and seek for guidance. Some are healed by the prayer of faith, and if one, why not another; if some, why not all? I have searched the Scriptures from end to end again and again that I might know the truth, and I have not found the subject easy of solution.

The Problem of Divine Healing

There is healing through the prayer of faith. The truth of this is confirmed by many witnesses who are both sane and saintly. There are those to whom is given the gift of healing, and they lay hands upon the sick and they recover. I myself have been healed through the prayer of faith. In my ministry I have been used of God to the healing of the sick. I have never exercised the ministry of healing except at the urgent request of the sick and a sure constraint of the Spirit of God. In other cases I have been quite helpless. There are those for whom I would have given my right hand if I could have prayed them to health, but I have had to see them suffer and die. Some have suffered untold anguish of mind because they sought for healing in vain. That has been my problem. While I was yet a young minister, one of the workers of the church was stricken with disease. We claimed the promises, and some of the best people I have ever known prayed earnestly and believingly for his recovery. We refused to believe that faith could fail. He died while we prayed. The shock to our faith was overwhelming. A sister of my own was an invalid for many years. Devout souls distressed her by the arguments Job's comforters had hurled at him. Together we searched the Scriptures and inquired of the Lord, beseeching Him that she might be healed. The Lord answered her in a vision and gave her peace, but not healing. I could multiply such instances on the one side and on the other, and it may be that others have been similarly perplexed.

Witnesses of Divine Healing

There are many witnesses that the Lord is our Healer. A few years ago I was in the neighborhood of Bishop Auckland, where Pastor Jeffries had held a mission some months before. As we were leaving the house where we had called, one of our party expressed regret to her sister that she had not brought some special tablets for her. She had been a martyr to severe pains in the head for years, and this was some new remedy to be tried. She answered gaily, "You needn't bring them. My head doesn't need them. The Lord healed me and I have never had a suspicion of pain since." Her husband and children confirmed her testimony with the remark: "She is a different woman." There are many such witnesses. The most remarkable example of divine healing I have known took place at the Southport Convention. The Rev. W. H. Tindall was president of the convention, and the strain of much speaking had brought on a disease of the throat. For more than a year he had not spoken above a whisper and even that was painful. The specialists gave no hope of recovery. At all the meetings he was a pathetic and silent figure. Prayer was offered for him continually. At the speaker's prayer meeting on the Friday morning there was a remarkable intensity and unity of faith. No one could pray for anything but the recovery of Mr. Tindall's voice. Faith gathered courage, forgot impossibilities, and claimed the promise. Dr. Ebenezer E. Jenkins presided, and when the rest of us rose from our knees Mr. Tindall remained kneeling. Dr. Jenkins said, "This is the most remarkable prayer meeting I have ever known," and placing his hand on the president's head he declared, in the name of the Lord, that we would hear Mr. Tindall speak in the tent before the convention closed. That night Mr. Tindall spoke in the tent for fifteen minutes and was heard by twelve hundred people, and he preached without loss of voice to the end of his days. I was present and saw and heard, and there are those still alive to confirm my testimony.

The experience of Stanley Jones as recorded in

The Christ of the Indian Road is another great illustration of the divine will and power to heal. Before the supreme missionary opportunity of his life he found himself spiritually impotent and physically broken. "I saw," he says, "that unless I got help from somewhere I would have to give up my missionary career, go back to America, and go to work on a farm to try to regain my health. It was one of my darkest hours. At that time I was in a meeting at Lucknow. While in prayer, not particularly thinking about myself, a Voice seemed to say, 'Are you yourself ready for this work to which I have called you?' I replied, 'No, Lord, I am done for. I have reached the end of my rope.' The Voice replied, 'If you will turn that over to me and not worry about it, I will take care of it.' I quickly answered, 'Lord, I close the bargain right here.' A great peace settled into my heart and pervaded me. I knew it was done! Life—abundant life—had taken possession of me. . . . For days after that I hardly knew I had a body. I went through the days, working all day and far into the night, and came down to bedtime wondering why in the world I should ever go to bed at all, for there was not the slightest trace of tiredness of any kind. I seemed possessed by Life and Peace and Rest—by Christ Himself. . . . Nine of the most strenuous years of my life have gone by since then, and the old trouble has never returned, and I have never had such health. I seemed to have tapped new life for body, mind and spirit. Life was on a permanently higher level. And I have done nothing but take it."

The Rev. Andrew Murray had a very similar experience. After he was healed, he traveled for several years extensively in Europe, America, and South Africa, preaching and speaking daily with great powers; and yet when ill, towards the close of his life, he said to his daughter in a voice full of tender sweetness: "My child, I would so much like to hold evangelistic meetings, but God does not see fit to heal me."

What Saith the Scripture?

The teaching of the Scriptures is the final authority on this subject, as on every other question of faith and life. The teaching of the Bible is for me the last word. I accept it whether I understand it or not. Faith can wait. It is humbling to have to bear the reproachful pity of those who speak with the confident authority of science and philosophy, learning and psychology, but the yoke of Christ is easy when faith is assured and meekness is content to wait God's time. When evolution and revelation seem to be at variance, faith banks with revelation. The difficulty is not, however, with the hostility of science and learning, but with the contradictions among those who believe. There are differences of interpretation, but we may leave the disputants to their contentions and seek to know the truth for ourselves as far as we can.

There is no doubt that the Scriptures teach that *the Lord is our Healer.* That is one of the names by which He is revealed. It is also beyond dispute that our Lord and Saviour regarded healing as an integral part of His ministry. He was a Physician who healed without medicine all kinds of diseases. He commissioned His apostles to heal the sick. The gift of healing was, and is, among the gifts of the Spirit. Healing was part of the apostolic ministry. The gift has never been withdrawn from the Church. Through all the ages there have been witnesses to its power. The promise in the Epistle of James is for all time: "The prayer of faith shall save the sick, and the Lord shall raise him up; and if he have committed sins, they shall be forgiven him."

The Bible associates sickness with Satan. God did not make man to be sick. Sickness came with sin. Jesus attributed some sicknesses to the devil. He said of one woman that Satan had bound her eighteen years (Luke 13:16). In Acts 10:38 we read that "Jesus went about doing good and healing the diseases of all who were oppressed of the devil." At the same time, He rebuked those who traced sickness and calamity to personal sinfulness. "Neither hath this man sinned nor his parents, that he should be born blind."

Sickness and sin are associated in redemption and healing. St. Matthew sees in the healing ministry of our Lord the fulfillment of Isaiah's prophecy. "He cast out the spirits with a word, and healed all that were sick; that it might be fulfilled which was spoken by Isaiah the prophet, saying, Himself took our infirmities, and bare our diseases" (Matt. 7:16–17). He bore our sicknesses as He bore our sins, for they were part of the same burden. It cannot mean that they were transferred to Him, for, so far as we know, He was never sick, but in sympathy and at great cost in physical and mental virtue He lifted their burden and bore it away. The sickless Christ bore our sickness, as the sinless Christ bore our sins. When He healed the palsied man who was let down through the roof, He began with his sin. Others whom He healed He commanded to sin no more, and the passage in James links healing with forgiveness. There is a passage of St. Paul's (1 Cor. 11:27–30) that traces sickness and even death to spiritual dishonor.

There is sickness in which there is no sin. It may be true theologically that all sickness came from sin, but experientially there is a sickness that is of grace. Scripture must interpret scripture. The affliction of Job was of grace. It was to the glory of God. Paul's thorn in the flesh was not of sin. Satan took advantage of it, but God gave it for the glory of His grace. Paul healed others, but he accepted his own sufferings as part of the afflictions of Christ. Epaphroditus was healed by the Lord (Phil. 2:27), Trophimus he had to leave at Miletus sick (2 Tim. 4:20); for Timothy's stomach he recommended a moderate use of wine (1 Tim. 5:23), and on his travels there went with him Luke, the beloved physician.

I Believe in Divine Healing

I believe in the healing power of faith. Apart from religion there is, generally speaking, health for the man who lives by faith. Sickness is of the mind rather than of the flesh. Divine healing is more than healing by faith. It is not to be confused with hypnotism and autosuggestion. The Lord is the Healer. The faith is in Him. The grounds of my faith are in Him. I trust

His Word, the redeeming work of Christ, and the sanctifying power of His Spirit who quickens our mortal bodies. The main concern is to know the will of God. Sickness may be chastisement for dis-obedience, and by faith the cause may be removed, the sin forgiven, and health restored. I am bound to believe that sickness may be in the will of God, for the purpose of discipline, for the glory of His grace, and for demonstrating the ministry of Christ.

I am sure that divine healing is a fact; and that the gift of healing waits within the Church for the prayer of faith.

I am sure that many people are sick who ought never to have been sick, and who might now be healed.

I am sure that no life is so health-giving and so radiant as the life of joyous and obedient faith.

I am sure I believe with all my heart and mind in divine healing, in spite of the fact that I am often ailing.

16

The Problem of
Unanswered Prayer

IT IS many years since I first wrote on Unanswered Prayer. The problem became acute when the man for whom we were praying so earnestly and confidently died while we prayed. The shock of it was overwhelming. It had never occurred to us that he might die. We had claimed the promise. We were absolutely sure of the Word. I do not think my faith was ever so sorely tried. We went back to the Word, and God gave me a message that has brought consolation to many, and through all the years it has been a stronghold for my trust. Many years have passed since then, but the truth abides, and though it may involve some repetition, I want to pass on the message to others.

The Problem

There can be no doubt that God answers prayer. On this point the Scriptures speak plainly enough.

Nothing could be more definite. All men are commanded to pray, at all times, in all places, and for all needs. Assurances abound that prayer is heard. The promises are explicit, and the Scriptures are full of examples and encouragement. Christ's own word is, "Every one that asketh receiveth" (Matt. 7:8). The scope of the promise is without limit of place (1 Tim. 2:8), time (Luke 18:1), or subject (John 16:23; Matt. 21:22; Phil. 4:6). Everything that concerns man is of interest to God, and is a proper subject for prayer. God does not divide our needs into sacred and secular, spiritual and material. He who taught us to pray for the forgiveness of our sins taught us also to say, "Give us this day our daily bread."

Yet, as we have studied the subject, it has been made clear that there are conditions and limitations. There are laws of prayer. The unrestricted promises are hedged about with conditions. We are commanded to pray for all men, but there were some for whom the prophet was forbidden to pray (Jer. 7:16, see also 1 John 5:15–16). It is possible to ask and not receive (Ps. 66:18; James 4:2–3). Prayers that lack sincerity and faith cannot be heard. This is obvious. God judges by the heart. So do we. No one grants requests where these simple elements are wanting. The sincerity must extend to both petition and petitioner. Eloquence is not prayer (Isa. 29:13; John 9:31; James 4:6; 1 John 3:22).

Are All the Sincere, Earnest, Believing Prayers of Good People Granted?

The answer of experience is, No. I have seen a distracted mother cling to the corpse of her child, refusing to believe it was dead. She had prayed. God had promised. She had believed. He heard, always heard. How could her child die? When at last the truth has forced itself upon her protesting mind, the distress deepens at the thought that God has not heard. There are many such days of desperate faith. Is God angry, as in the case of David (2 Sam. 12:14–23), even though there can be no such cause? Can it be that He is indifferent? Can it be that He does not know? Has He forgotten? Is it any use to pray? It was with such thoughts as these that I turned to my Bible and found the answer in three respective cases:

1. Deut. 3:23–27, where Moses prayed that he might go over into Canaan.

2. 1 Kings 19:4. Elijah's prayer that he might die.

3. 2 Cor. 12:8–9, in which Paul prayed for the removal of affliction.

These three men occupy a prominent place in Scripture, and yet each was denied his request. Their prayers are fairly representative and cover the ground of the problem.

The Prayer of Moses

Moses prayed that he might be allowed to complete his work. He had undertaken it at God's command. For forty years he had nursed and led a murmuring and ungrateful people through the wilderness. The promised land was within sight. What more natural than that he should desire to see his life-work completed? Besides, to all human judgment he could not be spared. He would be needed in Canaan

even more than in the wilderness. There were enemies
to be driven out, the constitution to be established,
and the people to be settled. If he should leave them
now, the work of forty years would fall to pieces.
Internal strife would wreck the nation. No wonder he
prayed that he might go over. In spite of a nation's
entreaty, regardless of his record, and notwithstanding
his earnest pleading, he died; died with his work
unfinished; died when he seemed to be most needed;
died with the hope of years at last within his reach.

Is it not often so?

A lifework is accepted as a divine appointment.
The powers of brain and muscle, time and energy, all
a man is goes into the task at the cost of personal
comfort and ambition. You pray for your work, that
God will prosper it and bless you in it. That is right.
No man has a right to be in any business for which he
cannot pray. God does not put a man into business
for worthless or unworthy ends. He means the work
to prosper; and yet how often it happens that the
prayers of good men seem to fail. Plans over which
they have prayed collapse. Competitors prevail.
Misfortune overwhelms. Ill health disables. Death calls,
and the work of years is left unfinished. Death at such
times seems almost spiteful in its cruelty. It strikes the
arm as it stretches the hand to grasp the prize; takes
the parent and counselor when he can least be spared;
passes by the weak and takes the strong; strikes down
the burden-bearer and spares the burden. We plead
that we may stay a little longer: only a little while; just
till this is completed; just till the children are grown
up or the business settled; and the answer is, "Get thee

up into the top of Pisgah"—and die. David wanted to build a house for God. His heart was set on it. God praised him for wanting to do it, but He forbade him (1 Chron. 22:8). So is many a heart set with a yearning that prays and aches for a work that is withheld. The Gadarene man Jesus saved with a mighty salvation prayed that he might go with Jesus, and Jesus sent him home (Luke 8:38).

Juniper Tree Prayers

Elijah was mighty in prayer. God answered all his prayers but one, and that was the prayer that he might die. He was under the juniper tree, suffering from mental and physical reaction. Yesterday had been a great day. He had stood alone as God's champion: strong, defiant, triumphant. The next day was the day after! At the threat of a woman he fled. His nerves were unstrung. Fear, despondency and despair took hold of him. In the fret and frenzy of depression he prayed that he might die. The disease is still with us, and is so multiplied that there are not enough juniper trees to go around. There are morbid Christians who have built tabernacles under them. Nerve collapse is more spiritual than physical, though it is usually both. There is no despondency in faith. What a mercy God does not always take us at our word. Nothing dishonors God more than the fretful despondency of the saints. Juniper trees make poor sanctuaries.

The Apostle's thorn in the flesh need not detain us, for we have already dealt with the subject of prayer and affliction. The thorn was a physical affliction, and

because he regarded it as a hindrance he prayed for
its removal. It was not removed though he besought
the Lord thrice. He had to learn that affliction may be
God's messenger as well as the messenger of Satan.

The Answer to Unanswered Prayers

None of these prayers was unanswered. They were
not granted, but they were answered, and "No" was
the answer. "No" is as truly an answer as "Yes." When
a request is refused, it is truly as answered as when it is
granted. Refusal may be the only answer possible to
love and wisdom and truth. A child may cry for a razor,
and full-grown people may cry for things equally
unsuitable, unsafe and unwise. Many have lived to
thank God that He withstood their agonizing entreaties
at some particular time or for some particular thing
that seemed indispensable.

God never refuses without reason. He knows the
past, in which there may be reasons for present
disqualification. Forgiven sin may disable. Moses and
David were both examples of this (Deut. 32:49–52;
2 Sam. 12:14). There are vessels that break on the
wheel, and though another may be made, the original
is impossible. Diseases may be healed, but a lost limb
cannot be restored. The Lord knows the future as well
as the past. The immediate may imperil the future.
The eagerness for a mess of pottage may involve the
loss of an inheritance. Esau got the answer to his
entreaty at dinnertime. Jacob got his at dawn. God
spared Hezekiah fifteen years, but he had better have
gone when the Lord sent for him.

The Greater Includes the Less

Delays are not denials, and it pays to wait God's time. Moses got into Canaan, and Elijah went to heaven by a more glorious way than that of the juniper tree. No inspired prayer of faith is ever refused. "No" is never God's last word. If the prayer seems unanswered, it is because it is lost in the glory of the answer when it comes. God may refuse the route because He knows a better, and He took Moses into Canaan by a better way and in better company. I have known other people who have had to go by way of heaven to find the answer to their prayers. He took Elijah to heaven by a much more wonderful way than that of the grave. He wanted to die, and God gave His tired servant sleep and rest, and sent him away to the hills for a holiday. That is His remedy for nerves: a change of air, a new vision, and a bigger job. Paul never had any use for juniper trees, and to him God said, "My grace is sufficient for thee," and He taught him to glory in affliction and adversity. In the experience that first sorely tried out faith, God sent help out of the darkness. Through the tears of a broken heart the vision came, and when the memorial card was sent it bore this text, which rebuked our unbelief, "He asked life of Thee, and Thou gavest it him, even length of days for ever and ever." So in Glory shall we find our prayers have been interpreted according to the infinite wisdom and eternal love of God our Father, who bids us pray.

Unanswered yet! The prayers your lips have pleaded
  In agony of heart these many years?
Does faith begin to fail? Is hope departing?
  And think you all in vain those falling tears?
Say not, the Father hath not heard your prayer,
  You shall have your desire—sometime—somewhere.

Unanswered yet! Though when you first presented
  This one petition at the Father's Throne
It seemed you could not wait the time of asking
  So urgent was the heart to make it known;
Though years have passed since then, do not despair
  The Lord will answer you—sometime—somewhere.

Unanswered yet! Nay, do not say ungranted,
  Perhaps your work is not wholly done.
The work began when first your prayer was uttered,
  And God will finish what He has begun.
If you will keep the incense burning there,
  His glory you shall see—sometime—somewhere.

Unanswered yet! Faith cannot be unanswered;
  Her feet are firmly planted on the Rock;
Amid the wildest storms she stands undaunted,
  Nor quails before the loudest thunder-shock.
She knows Omnipotence has heard her prayer,
  And cries, "It shall be done—sometime—somewhere."

E. B. Browning